SKETCH OF AN ESCALADE

A

PRACTICAL TREATISE

ON THE

ATTACK OF MILITARY POSTS,

VILLAGES,

INTRENCHMENTS, &c.;

INTENDED AS A SUPPLEMENT TO

"THE DEFENCE OF OUTPOSTS;"

WITH A FAMILIAR EXPLANATION OF THE

PRINCIPLES AND PRACTICE OF ESCALADING.

By J. JEBB, c.b.,
Lieut.-Colonel Royal Engineers, &c.

SECOND EDITION.

The Naval & Military Press Ltd

Published by

The Naval & Military Press Ltd
Unit 5 Riverside, Brambleside
Bellbrook Industrial Estate
Uckfield, East Sussex
TN22 1QQ England

Tel: +44 (0)1825 749494

www.naval-military-press.com
www.nmarchive.com

In reprinting in facsimile from the original, any imperfections are inevitably reproduced and the quality may fall short of modern type and cartographic standards.

TO THE

SUBALTERNS

OF

THE BRITISH ARMY,

THIS LITTLE TREATISE,

DESIGNED TO ASSIST THEM IN THE ACQUIREMENT

OF A PRACTICAL KNOWLEDGE OF

AN IMPORTANT DUTY,

IS INSCRIBED BY

A BROTHER OFFICER.

PREFACE.

It being in contemplation to print a Second Edition of a little Work I published last year on the Defence of Outposts, &c., it has been suggested to me by a Military Friend, that in confining myself to the *Defence*, I have left "half the tale untold;"—inasmuch as it is of equal importance that a knowledge of the *Attack* of Military Posts should be acquired.

Indeed it is obvious enough, that the Attack and Defence will, under all circumstances, exercise a reciprocal influence upon each other, and that to execute *either*, with all the advantages of which they may be susceptible, a knowledge of *both* is essential. It is by knowing what power the Assailants really have in their hands, and how they can use it, that an Officer is competent to prepare and arrange his Defensive measures, and is enabled to foresee and meet such exigencies as may arise in the heat of Action; and the converse of this is equally true, an Officer cannot properly direct an Attack until he can form a just estimate of the difficulties he has to contend with, and the means which the Defenders can bring into play against him.

In the hope of throwing a little light on this subject, I hastily wrote the following pages, intending to add them to the Second Edition before alluded to, but as they have rather exceeded the limits I expected, and from other causes, it has been decided to publish them separately, as Parts I. and II.; with the further view of adding Part III., explanatory of the Attack of Fortresses, and of the very important Duties which the Officers and Men of the Line are called upon to perform, in the superintendence or execution of the Works of a Siege, when opportunity permits.

Whilst on the subject of the Attack of Intrenchments, &c., briefly treated of in the following sheets, I naturally stumbled upon Escalading, and have devoted a few pages to a little explanation of its principles and practice, to which I have added a few suggestions respecting it. This mode of Attack is not generally understood, in consequence of the limited opportunities which Officers have of acquainting themselves with its merits; and it is the more to be regretted, for an Escalade may justly be considered one of the most powerful and attainable means of assaulting Works, and is also one of general application.

Escalading on a more extended scale than had been attempted on Service, was organised into a system, and introduced by Colonel Pasley, at Chatham, in the year 1822; and by a subsequent Order from the Horse Guards, the different Regiments and Depôts, which successively pass through that Garrison to India and elsewhere, are regularly exercised in it by him, with manifest decision and effect. The benefit of this training was felt in the Burmese War, where some European Troops,* which had been practised previous to leaving England, bore a conspicuous part in the Escalade and Capture of the numerous formidable Stockades which constituted the bulwarks of the Burman Empire, and which until then had been deemed impregnable by their Defenders.

I must deprecate the criticism which may too justly be passed, on the levity of style by which the serious subjects I have attempted to explain are occasionally illustrated, and which I am "free to confess" is extremely *disrespectful* to them; but I fall back on "good intentions." My business is with the Subalterns of the Army, who, as a body, are not quite so *studious* as they might be; and if I have been fortunate enough to convey a little information in a form that they *will read*, my object, which is a sincere desire for the good of the Service, is attained.

Those who so gloriously gained personal experience in supporting the honour of the British Arms in our late Wars, are ebbing fast with the tide of Time from our Ranks, and it does not much exceed the limits of probability, to say, that the Subalterns who figure in the Army List of this month of June 1837, may be the Commanders of Regiments or Brigades when next we draw an hostile sword; and into their hands will then be confided the high character and unsullied reputation of the British Army. Circumstanced, therefore, as we are in this respect, it behoves the Junior Officers of the Service not to confine their views to the present moment, but to look forward to the time when they may have to aquit themselves of the highest responsibilities, and to prepare accordingly.

Their inherent Bravery, and ther *latent* Military Spirit and Genius, none can doubt, for they come of the same Stock as those Veterans who

---

* The 13th Light Infantry, which so much distinguished itself in that War was practised in Escalading at Chatham in 1822, and that gallant Officer, Major, (now Lieut.-Colonel) Sale, whose name stands so prominent in the heroic Enterprises in which they were engaged, was particularly active on that occasion.

have already shown what they are made of. *Blood* always has told, and always will!—but in order that we may take the Field again, with such an Army as we quitted it,—such an Army be it remembered, as the Sun seldom shines upon,—it is absolutely necessary that this Military Genius should not sleep through these piping times of Peace. It should be cultivated, encouraged, and matured, by every Officer and Man who has a just sense of what is due to the Service, and who enters it with the determination of being a *Soldier*.

In future Wars few will start with any EXPERIENCE, nor can that be obtained until there is opportunity; but the next best thing, which is KNOWLEDGE, is within the reach of all who choose to take the trouble of acquiring it. What Nelson said will bear repeating,—" ENGLAND EXPECTS EVERY MAN TO DO HIS DUTY!" But it may be added, it is an essential condition that he should first KNOW HOW!

J. J.

CHATHAM, 1837.

PREFACE TO THE SECOND EDITION.

In reprinting this little Treatise, I would willingly have endeavoured to do more justice to subjects I have attempted to explain, but not having had the opportunity of doing so, I must trust that the object I first had in view in drawing attention to these duties, in the disguise of what is called " a popular form," will excuse the shortcomings of the performance. This, therefore, is a Second Edition without the usual advantage, so much needed, of " considerable corrections and additions."

J. JEBB.

London,
14th June, 1848.

CONTENTS.

CHAPTER I.

OBSERVATIONS ON THE ATTACK OF OUTPOSTS—Sketch by a French Author of an irresistible ATTACK, and of an equally unconquerable DEFENCE—Of Attacks by SURPRISE, and by OPEN FORCE—Requisite information to be obtained previous to the Attack of a Village, or an Isolated Military Post, &c. 1

CHAPTER II.

FURTHER CONSIDERATIONS AND DETAILS—General Dispositions for the Attack of Works or Intrenchments, &c.—Principles which regulate them discussed and explained—Real and False Attacks—Advantages resulting from the Employment of Artillery—The two Assaults on Fort Christoval given as an Example 10

CHAPTER III.

SURMOUNTING OBSTACLES—How Infantry are to deal with an Abattis in an Attack by Surprise—How it is to be carried by Open Force—How other Impediments, such as Military Pits, &c., are to be passed—How Stockades, Ditches, Palisades, Chevaux de Frise, are to be surmounted or destroyed 29

CHAPTER IV.

OF ATTACKS BY SURPRISE—Circumstances which will admit of, or facilitate, this mode of Attack—Various considerations which ought to be weighed in determining the point—Of the *Time* most favourable for surprising a Post, and circumstances which influence the selection—Of the advantages and disadvantages of Night Attacks—Proportionate number of men for making an Attack—Requisite precautions—Division of the Force—Order of the March, and DISTRIBUTION OF THE ASSAILANTS—Specific orders they should receive—Conduct and precautions during an Attack—Scaling a Wall or Stockade, &c.—BLOWING OPEN BARRIERS—Mode of applying a Bag of Powder for the purpose—Previous Dispositions—Precautions to be observed 32

CHAPTER V.

OF ATTACKS BY OPEN FORCE—Under what circumstances they are imposed—Requisite information to be obtained, and measures to be followed—In what points it differs from an Attack by SURPRISE—Precautions to be adopted, &c. 48

CHAPTER VI.

ATTACK OF AN INTRENCHED VILLAGE—General Sketch of Proceedings—Reconnoissance—Columns of Attack—Position of the Artillery, &c.—Arrangements for, and progress of the Affair—Reference to former Chapters for Detail . . 51

CONTENTS.

CHAPTER VII.

Page

ATTACK OF A FLECHE, OR EARTHEN WORK OPEN IN THE REAR—A REDOUBT, &c. Description of such Works—General Dispositions to be made, and precautions to be observed—Real and False Attacks, and their reciprocal influence upon each other—Capture of a Redoubt described by Captain Macaulay—Sir James Kempt's Assault on Fort Picurina given as an Example 56

CHAPTER VIII.

ATTACK OF A FORTIFIED BUILDING—Requisite information to be obtained—Precautions to be observed, and mode of proceeding—Distribution of the Force, and formation of the Columns for a supposed Attack—Breaking through the Barricades by the explosion of a Bag of Powder—Attack, by an Escalade of the Windows—Silencing Loopholes by superior numbers—Forcing an Entrance, and subsequent Dispositions—Scaling the Roof, and making the Attack from above, &c. 62

CHAPTER IX.

ESCALADING—An explanation of its Principles and Practice—A supposed attempt to Escalade in Column, and the practical working of such a system—Its hopeless result—True Principle of an Attack by Escalade discussed in a familiar manner—Defence of the great Breach at Badajos—Supposed Assault of a great Outwork—Progress of an Escalade in Line, and explanation of its probable effects—Suggestions for enabling the Assailants to regain the formation of Columns during the Attack—Change in the arrangements when the number of Ladders is limited—Mode of proceeding with an insufficient supply—How to proceed with *still less* than an insufficient supply—Lord Hill's Escalade and Capture of the Works at Almarez, given as an Example—The End . . . 71

ON THE ATTACK OF OUTPOSTS.

CHAP. I.—OBSERVATIONS ON THE ATTACK OF OUTPOSTS, VILLAGES, INTRENCHMENTS, &c.

AFTER the endeavour to show in PART I. on the "*Defence of Outposts*," how impregnable a Military Post may be made by the judicious application of a very little labour, there is certainly an awkwardness attending the addition of a Supplementary Document, to prove the extraordinary facility with which they may be attacked, and how easy it is to overcome all the boasted Obstacles, and vanquish the Defenders. Interested in a subject, a Writer is insensibly led on to make out as good a case as a regard for truth and the common sense of others will permit; in doing which he may perhaps, without intending it, sometimes trench a little on the privileges of the Special Pleader. If He of the three-tailed Wig, after having said his say on one side, should have a Brief handed over to him from the opposite one, he would have to go to the "right about;" and the extent of his predicament in a second time showing "the "*worse* to be the *better* cause," would depend upon the solidity of his former statements; and an enlightened Jury would have to balance the merits and evidence on both sides, and judge for themselves about the Verdict. An eminent French Author, who flourished not 100 years ago, when placed in this same dilemma, assumes rather an amusing attitude, and as he makes a capital Fight of it

B

both ways, and moreover conveys a very instructive lesson in his animated sketches of the Attack and Defence of a Redoubt, it will need no apology for plunging at once "*in Medias Res*," by inserting the substance of them here, for in doing so we shall acquire a general notion of the subject to start with. He delivers himself to the following effect :—

" *Of the Attack.*

" If the Redoubt is of small importance, and unprovided with Artillery, it may be attacked without much preamble. The Light Troops envelop it, keeping up a shower of well-directed balls, on the crest of the parapet, to prevent the enemy showing themselves. They approach by little and little, under cover of any irregularities of the ground that may offer. They get up any trees that the enemy have been fools enough to leave standing, from whence they can see into the Work and select their victims; by particular desire giving the Officers the preference, especially him who appears to be Chief. This converging fire so belabours the parapet and gives such a superiority, that it makes it quite a pleasant march as far as any Obstacle that may be placed in front of the counterscarp, or even to the very edge of the ditch, if no Obstructions have been placed. In the latter case they may jump into the Ditch (the depth is not stated,) without deliberation, and prepare for the Assault; one party remaining above to continue the fire against any one daring to show himself. After taking breath at the bottom of the Ditch, they give the Assault, for which purpose the leading files are shoved up by their comrades as far as the Berm, and from thence by a fresh effort they scramble up the

Exterior slope,—arrive at the top,—fire down on the people,—jump into the work,—pursue the Defenders '*la Baionette dans les reins*,' and force them to surrender.

"This will do for a *little one*, but for a great Redoubt or Fort armed with Artillery, provided with an interior Intrenchment, and with an Abattis, '*Trous de loup*,' &c. on the outside, the dispositions for the attack would be otherwise.

"First of all, a Reconnoisance would be necessary, in order that preparations might be made for ensuring success. Batteries for Enfilade, and others for Direct fire, would be constructed during the night, and some pieces would be specially directed against the Gates, to deprive the enemy of all hope of escape. With the dawn of day, the fire commences; the Howitzers enfilade the Lines, —belabour the parapets,—breach the palisades,—damage the abattis,—destroy the artillery, and inundate the terreplein with Shells. The Direct batteries, armed with Cannon, thunder away and pulverize the embrasures,— dismount the guns, and put the greater part of the Gunners *hors de combat*. When this is accomplished, the Light Troops rush forward and cover the work with their fire, whilst the Troops of the Line, formed into as many Columns as there are Salients to attack, begin to show themselves. The drums beat the the charge,—the ground trembles under the tread of these Warriors, who are only impatient for the combat: they arrive at the Abattis, which forces them to halt until some Sappers, who have marched at their head, have cleared away this obstacle. They reply not to the fire; the Light Troops must do that part of the business—the way is open to them: the columns again advance,—the leading files throw planks (which have hitherto served them as bucklers) upon the *Trous de loup*, and a road is made which only hastens the desired instant of personal contact. The Ditch, deep though it may be, checks not the ardour of the Grenadiers; down they go into it,—upset the palisades (if there are any),—take breath after their exertions, and give the Assault. The glory is to him who first dies on the top. (Odds,—laurels! —what a satisfaction!) Numbers expire, victims to their ardour; the rest burn to avenge their memory; and after more or less resistance, the Flag of the Assailant unfurls itself on the highest point of the Fort. The Defenders, overcome by numbers, have retired into their Retrenchment, and demand a Capitulation : the generous Victor refuses it not; he knows how to appreciate a brave defence, and so far from ill-treating an Enemy, whom he esteems, grants him conditions,—fraternises uncommon,—overwhelms him with kindness, and consoles him with his praises."

So much for that,—from which the miserable and utterly hopeless condition of the gallant Defenders of a respectable Work may be gleaned. Now for the Defence,—What can these poor devils possibly do to save themselves? *On verra!*

"*Defence of a Redoubt.*

"The Officer who receives the honour of defending a Post of importance '*a l'outrance*,' should neglect no means of inspiring the brave men who are to share with him the dangers of an heroic resistance, and the Laurels which will crown their brows, when they are conducted in triumph before their General, if they arrest the progress of the enemy. He should fortify their *Morale* by putting a good face upon it, and by a gaiety of manner he should communicate a spark of that fire which animates his own breast. It is by extolling their prowess and recalling their former deeds; it is by giving the Laurels, which already adorn their brows, 'a bit of a shake,' and tickling their ears with glorious names and recollections of their country, that he 'gets their steam up.' He should persuade them that they are all heroes, inaccessible to fear, and that though an enemy may vanquish, he can never force them to surrender. '*Foris victores Domi invincabiles*' is the motto he nails to his Standard.

"The Hour, that is to try what they are made of, arrives, —already some Skirmishers of the Enemy appear in the distance,—groups begin to form in the horizon, and a cloud of dust rising and gradually approaching along the main road, at length vomits forth on the Plain the heavy Columns of the Assailants which it envelops. At this moment the Guns of the Fort should be directed on the Masses, and if any one hazards a nearer approach, he should be assailed with Musketry, giving him ten shots rather than one.

"The Attack will probably be delayed till next morning. At daylight the enemy opens his fire, which must be replied to as warmly as possible; but this distant combat will not be of long duration; the Enemy impatient to overcome the obstacles which arrest his progress, sends forth his Light Troops. They are kept at a distance by showers of Grape shot. They approach again, and begin seriously to disturb the Gunners, who retire accordingly, and give place to the Infantry, who prepare to line the parapet: a species of calm reigns for a moment, and the Light Troops gain the abattis. The fire of musketry is directed upon them. Showers of balls riddle the boldest who have dared to attempt to get over that obstacle, numbers of them bite the dust, the others 'make themselves scarce,' and this first success encourages the Defenders. The Chief retires his Soldiers into the interior of the Work to prepare for a more terrible attack. He alone remains exposed, observing with the utmost *sang froid* what passes. He sees the Masses coming on, and gives the order for the Artillery to exterminate them. They devote themselves to that particular service with the resolution that their fire shall not cease till they have accomplished it. (Pleasant fellows!)

"These formidable Masses advance like a Storm driving before a horrible tempest. A cloud of Light Troops accompany them; already they touch the Abattis, and the axe is at work to clear a road through it. The whole of the Defenders rise at once;— the fire opens again and is maintained without intermission upon them. The Enemy fatigued by his efforts retires beyond its reach to take breath: each time he touches our first bulwark he is checked by our redoubled Fire: we have the superiority and we profit by it. His loss is enormous but he regards it not, and brings up fresh Troops, and as he thus rises like a Phœnix from her ashes, he again presents a formidable front and an imposing Force.

"Our external means of defence yield at length to the Enemy: we hear him throw himself into the Ditch; already we are menaced by his fury, but there remains for us the brightest hopes. Some of the Defenders throw a shower of Grenades; others with difficulty lifting the largest Stones, hurl them over the parapet and crush the Assailants. Everything favours us in this unequal contest:

we wait for our adversaries with firmness, and as they, with difficulty, crawl up the slope under the weight of their Arms, with one blow we send them spinning from the top to the bottom, and in their fall they carry with them all those who were behind them. Having cleared our Parapet a second time, we cover those below with Stones and Grenades. The Ditch begins to fill up with carcases. He hesitates—by Jove! he is going to take himself off! Hope animates us afresh;—joy redoubles;—our ardour and our last shots accompany the last of our enemies: there they go like a rabble! We celebrate our Victory with Songs of Triumph;—we repair our breaches;—we bestow a tear or two *en passant* on our companions who have paid their tribute to their country, and here come the Battalions who advance to the rescue!"

These exhilarating descriptions of Attack and Defence, though they leave us a little in doubt which side is likely to have the best of it, and have besides a dash of the marvellous about them, nevertheless give a good outline of the Principles and Practice which each party would follow.

He must have been a lively and desperate fellow, that old Writer!! One can fancy him a little Man with a longish back, (they are always valorous,) with a big cocked hat in his hand, haranguing his brave fellows—" considerable magniloquent"—directing their energies with wisdom; leading them on to glory—and afterwards either stretched a grim corpse on the reeking field of his exertions, a cheerful sacrifice for the honour of his country, or if he should have lived through the hubbub, then doing the amiable to his vanquished foes. One may swear that the "*fortiter in re*," and the "*suaviter in modo*," were alike familiar to him.

But we must leave him blazing away, and endeavour to fill up his graphic sketches by a little more detail of the operations.

1. Temporary Works may be attacked by SURPRISE or by OPEN FORCE, and it will be necessary to obtain accurate information on several essential points before a decision can be made as to which mode will be the most judicious or practicable under the circumstances. For instance, previous to making any dispositions for an attack, either of a Village, an Intrenchment, or a smaller Military Post, a Commander should have some knowledge of the *Locale*—the nature of the Defences, and the strength of the Force occupying them. It should be ascertained whether they are left to fight their own Battle, or are in a situation to receive Support, and from whence that support is to come; how the Duty is done; what is the nature of the Ground around it; whether favourable for Concealment or otherwise; which are the shortest and best Roads to it, &c. &c.

2. If an Intrenched Village is to be attacked, it should be ascertained by what means the streets and roads leading into it have been closed; whether by Stockades or Breastworks—(Nos. 75 and 57, Part I.); how these Obstacles are flanked—whether from neighbouring houses, or temporary works thrown up for the purpose; what Obstructions are placed in front of them—whether Abattis, *Trous de loup,* (No. 78,) &c.; how the Houses forming points in the main enclosure have been strengthened; whether there is a Keep, (No. 121,) and of what nature it is,—and how fortified; whether there is any Building occupied on the outside as an Advanced Post; where the Picquets are placed, &c.

3. If the Post is an isolated Building, such as a Country House, or Church, (No. 90,) attention should be directed to the mode in which the Doors have been barricaded, or the Windows blocked up; how the Loop-holes are arranged; what sort of Flank defence has been obtained; how it can best be approached; what internal preparations have been made for prolonging the defence, &c. Part of this "useful knowledge" may be drawn from Spies, Deserters, and Maps, not however trusting any of them much further than they can be seen or verified; and for the rest, there is nothing comparable to seeing for one's self, and therefore either an open Reconnoisance, or a secret Peep must, somehow or other, be obtained.

4. These hints will suffice to show that there are a multiplicity of objects which require to be looked to, before an opinion can be formed as to the best course to pursue; and unless some previous information is obtained upon some or all of them, false calculations will necessarily be made, unexpected Obstacles will be encountered, and hazardous enterprises will be undertaken, all which might at least have been modified. With superior numbers in hand, and no very great show of opposition in front, it may be difficult to "hold hard" and exercise patience, but under most circumstances, there is wisdom in "craning a little bit," and just finding out what one has to encounter both before and behind the little level lines of Parapets and Palings which look so inviting "for a Lark." There may be some great yawning Ditch, which it is not so easy to take "in your stride." And things are not always quite so smooth as they look; it is therefore better to find out if you can, and prepare accordingly.

CHAP. II.—FURTHER CONSIDERATIONS AND DETAILS.

5. The Dispositions for the attack, of whatever nature it may be, though they require to be made with great circumspection and executed with the utmost celerity, decision and effect, do not perhaps call for so many precautions as are necessary for the Defence of a Work. It is with the Assailants, to choose what they will do; with the Defenders,—on very short notice, to conform and make the best of it. The first object of an Attack is to get *at*, the people who are defending a Work, and then—*to beat them*. To secure the former, a Commander would naturally seek for a point which presented the fewest Obstacles, and when he saw where to strike the Blow, he would accomplish the latter, by hitting "uncommon hard;" so hard as to make his Adversary reel under it, if it did not knock him head over heels, and get rid of him altogether. These main objects being kept in view, everything that would conduce to secure them must be studied and carried into effect. He would therefore arrange his plan with the utmost Caution, and execute it with corresponding Vigour. It will be obvious, that where it is practicable, several real Attacks, or one *Leviathan*, and several false ones, will distract an Enemy's attention,—divide his Forces,—tend to disturb him and shake his confidence,—render his combinations more perplexing, and in short give him more to attend to, with diminished means of doing it, than if one attack only were made. It is usual, therefore, where circumstances permit, to attack several points at the same moment, or in quick

succession. To effect this the Columns are formed under the nearest cover that can be found, from which they advance with as much celerity, as will leave the Men *fresh and in wind* when they get to work. To regulate even this properly is a point of no small importance. For instance, if a Column has any considerable distance to move, in the face of a smart peppering fire, and they start at too great a pace, they may be brought to a stand still, before they can close with their opponents, and that too when the fire upon them, from its diminished distance, is the more deadly. The means of moving *powerfully and swiftly at the last*, must be preserved at all events; besides all its other good effects, it is enlivening to go in "at a slapping place." This forward movement is covered by Light Infantry, who would halt on the outside of the Ditch or other Obstacle, and whilst the Column was engaged in getting over it, would endeavour by good steady shooting, to aid the operation in keeping down the Enemy's Fire, or putting "a stopper over all," or any overt acts of opposition on the part of the Defenders. No dancing about on the top a parapet allowed! It would be a weak proceeding to permit any of the men in the Column to amuse themselves by Firing; and, to prevent disappointment, it might be explained that they have much more serious business to attend to with the Bayonet, and till that is done, they should think of nothing else. Any little *decided leisure*, might be so employed by a few of the leading Files being disposed in front for that purpose, whilst the others were lying down to cover themselves; but the main point should never be lost sight of; no Time should be wasted upon it, for the Assailants and Defenders, under such circumstances, are far from being on equal terms; the former being exposed from top to toe all in the open, and the latter at the worst would be covered up to their chins.

6. Each Column designed for making an Attack is usually divided into Two parts, the relative strength of which must be determined by the nature of the Operation,—the number of the Defenders,—and a train of probabilities too long to be enumerated here. One party is for Storming the Work, and the other is placed in Reserve, to be applied as events turn out, either to assist in following up and taking advantage of success, or as "a friend in need" to fall back upon, in case of disaster. The former of these Parties may be again subdivided, into two or more parts; one for the first Onset, and the others for Support; but this should be more *nominal* than *real*. The Question is, shall we send the whole Storming Party on, in one Mass, or shall we first *start* it in separate Detachments, and then let it *finish* as one Mass? We require the Moral as well as the Physical effect which NUMBERS will produce, in order to penetrate the Enemy's line; but if we can secure those essentials when wanted, it does not appear necessary to expose the Support or the *Tail* of the Column, whilst any work is going on which the *Head* of it, or the real Storming Party, can effect just as well by itself. For instance, there would be little good gained by a vast Body of Men being halted under a close Fire, whilst Workmen were engaged in cutting a Road for them through Palisades or an Abattis, or whilst the leading Files were rearing Ladders for an Escalade, &c. The *Moral effect* and Confidence produced by *Numbers*, which it is most essential to study, would be still retained if the *Head* of a Column

could feel assured that it travelled with its *Tail* on, though it could not see it, and that however fast the one might move, the other would be certain to follow; and the *Physical effect* or *Force* that is required for an Onset, would be equally secured by the same means. Numbers are in either case the chief ingredient; the only thing to be considered is, the proper application of them. This is confessedly rather a nice point to manage, and such as it is more easy to theorise upon than to carry into effect; but if Troops are handy, and are accustomed to work together, and to be *sure* of each other "in sight and out of sight," and that their Efforts are directed by the hand of a Master, there does not appear to be any impossibilities attending its adjustment; at any rate the Principle, if true, is not falsified because the Practice is difficult. "When in doubt," however, "*win the trick*," says Hoyle: if, therefore, Men and Means are dubious, Measures should be of an opposite character: the lesser evil would be unquestionably to make sure of it, and start *One* Column, preceded by an advanced party of proportionate strength, rather than run the chance of *Two*, or more, not acting simultaneously. In Night Attacks, for example, it is especially necessary that all the arrangements should be the simplest possible,—and under such circumstances an undivided force would be preferable to risking a mistake being made in the administration of separate parts of it. Give them the whole Dose at once, taking care, as *Morrison* would say of his *Pills*, to let them have *enough*.

7. In carrying out the Principle of the Storming Party and its Support marching separately, we ought to find that as the leading Files of the former became engaged, or as

the Explosion took place which was to blow the Barrier to atoms, by which they were to enter a Work, the Supporting Column should be close at their heels,—to add their Weight to the first Shock,—to inspire Confidence,—join in the Cheers,—and be at hand to rectify anything that might happen to go wrong. These little delicacies cannot be brought within the precise limits of any Rule which shall be of general application, whether as respects Distance, or Time, or Pace, or anything else. It is the Commander who has the right kind of Head on his Shoulders, and an Eye that is good for something in it,—who can alone apply the Principle, and regulate them on the spot. As an illustration which will be understood by a select few, we may say the Support should be like a man's Second Horse,* in a quickish thing with Foxhounds, that has lasted as long as is pleasant. By some Rule which only the few know by heart, it should be brought up quite Fresh, as if nothing had happened, and be exactly in the *right place* at the *particular moment* when it is required. One more explanatory illustration, and this digression into which we have inadvertently been betrayed, ends. It takes " all sorts" of men and comprehensions to make up a World, and a homely Simile may sometimes convey an idea more forcibly than a rounded Period. We now address those who know how to use their Fists, as well as other things—the PRIVATES who fill the Ranks of our Army; for they

---

* A Second Horse, be it known, does not go the whole Run, but being ridden by a *particular sort of man*, is, by nice management, made to " *nick in*" at the critical moment when his Owner could not go much further without him : and under circumstances when probably his weight in Gold, or all the Eyes of every Jew that ever was born, would not purchase him.

OBSERVATIONS ON ATTACK OF OUTPOSTS.   15

too ought to understand what they have to trust to, seeing they have rather a conspicuous part to play. The Storming Party is your Left Hand, the Support is your Right, and your Adversary is before you: you are not going to touch the " Light Guitar," but to knock him over. Therefore get your fingers into Close Column,—hit him straight in the Face with your Left fist, and Double him up with your Right. Do you understand that? Yes! Then when you have an opportunity practise it, and don't be ashamed to hit as hard as you can when you are about it!

8. Troops aided by Musketry in the manner adverted to in No. 5, would plant Ladders for Escalading; Sappers would cut away Palisades, blow open Barriers or Gates, make steps in Slopes that were too steep to be ascended, or clear away Impediments; and a steady Charge would then take place: not one Man running at the top of his speed with his Bayonet at a fellow's breech, and another after him; that is not the way to get rid of a set of resolute Fellows. It must be a steady Charge, or rather a quiet determined Rush; the whole Weight of the Column is wanted to make the desired impression in the Adversary's Line, and if it is frittered away bit by bit, much of the effect is expended in individual acts of Heroism, which might be more usefully employed. Where several Attacks are made, the Columns may as well all march on the same Front, of subdivisions, or a greater or less formation as might be convenient,—it will make it more difficult for an enemy to estimate numbers, or distinguish the Real from the False attacks; and the latter should look and act as if they intended Mischief, however innocent their designs may be. They should also be of such a Strength as to

command respect, and in order that they may be in a condition to profit by unforeseen success; the *number* of attacks should therefore be in proportion to the Force that is to be divided. How frequently has it happened, that a False Attack, which would have been considered as too rash and hazardous an Enterprise to be thought of seriously for a moment, has been crowned with a success which has equally astonished Friends and Foes; whilst others, which have been judiciously planned and organized, have altogether failed?

9. It is explained further on, in No. 23, that the "top o'the morning" is not a bad time for making an Assault; this is chiefly because the previous movements are concealed by the darkness, and the loss is diminished in proportion. For instance, under favourable circumstances, it would be quite possible, after driving in an Enemy's Picquets the preceding evening, secretly to dispose a Firing Party close to the Ditch on the outside of a Work, without a hostile shot being fired, for they are not always prepared for illuminating the exterior by Light balls, and to have a Column at no great distance waiting for the precise moment that was most favourable for the Attack; and when the Troops did advance for an Escalade, or whatever the operation might be,—what would happen? The Alarm would be given, and the Parapets would be manned; but opposed by a Firing Party, drawn up perhaps 3 deep within a distance, it might be of 20 or 30 yards,—who could show himself to give his fire? Let us see the man that would be long "in easy circumstances" with his head and shoulders above the Parapet! If Sandbags had been disposed for protecting the Defenders, a few shots might be fired through the Loopholes, but their effect would be as nothing. Only those directly

opposite a Column could be brought to bear at all at that distance, and with good arrangement there would be no Time for Mischief to ensue, even if there were more opportunity. An Attack thus favoured therefore, would secure to the Assailants most of the advantages of a Surprise, and is intermediate between a case of *amazement*, and one of *open hostility*.

10. Circumstances, however, will arise as stated in No. 40, when an undisguised Attack in broad daylight may be imposed, and like most other things in this life, it has some advantages to boast of, though they may be counterbalanced by a preponderance of Evils greater than attend more insidious proceedings. There is, of course, more previous *Exposure*, but people *See what they have to do*, and can therefore act with more decisive effect. In the preparatory movements, and during the advance of the Columns, Violence must, in this mode of attack, control Opposition, instead of its effects being eluded by Secrecy or Concealment. The employment of Light Troops and Artillery are the chief means which may be applied by the Assailants for effecting this object; the Former can act as a Firing Party under any circumstances in covering the advance, but it is quite necessary there should be Light enough in order to derive all the benefits which the latter can bestow. Artillery can effect that from a distance, which without it, Infantry would have to execute for themselves, under all the disadvantages of a close fire. Thus, by firing in a slanting direction at Stockade Work,—an Abbattis,—or Palisading, these Obstacles become so damaged and torn up, that a Passage improved by the use of the axe, is readily effected through them; Barriers may be knocked away

from Doors or Windows; Walls may be breached, or the Defenders in a Building may be very much incommoded by its effects—for shot will go through and through ordinary Houses, and if a lively fire be kept up, they soon cease to be comfortable quarters. By firing shells into Parapets, that portion which covers the Defenders may, if time admits, be partially got rid of; and when all these good things are effected from the Front, the Guns being moved to one of the Flanks, so as to obtain a general Enfilade, may keep up a fire till the moment of Assault, which will unsettle the Defenders, and ensure a corresponding advantage to the Attack: in fact, it is difficult to say what a Brigade of Horse Artillery or a Battery of 9-pounders *cannot do* against a Military Post fortified in haste, or indeed against anything else. With an overwhelming Force, backed by a powerful Artillery, it would be out of place to be so particular; a Victim would be well pounded from a distance, and then being attacked on all sides, the Defenders would not have much more to say for themselves: with a Force however only just adequate to the object, more caution, but equal boldness, would influence the proceedings.

11. The Principles on which Attacks are conducted, and the general arrangements for executing them, will be gleaned from the preceding pages; but in illustration of some of the Remarks, it may be useful to adduce an Example; and as such, the arrangements for, and the execution of, the two Assaults made on Fort Christoval, a large Outwork on the right bank of the Guadiana, opposite to the Castle of Badajos, during the Sieges of that Fortress in May and June 1811, as detailed by Sir John Jones, will

PLATE. I.

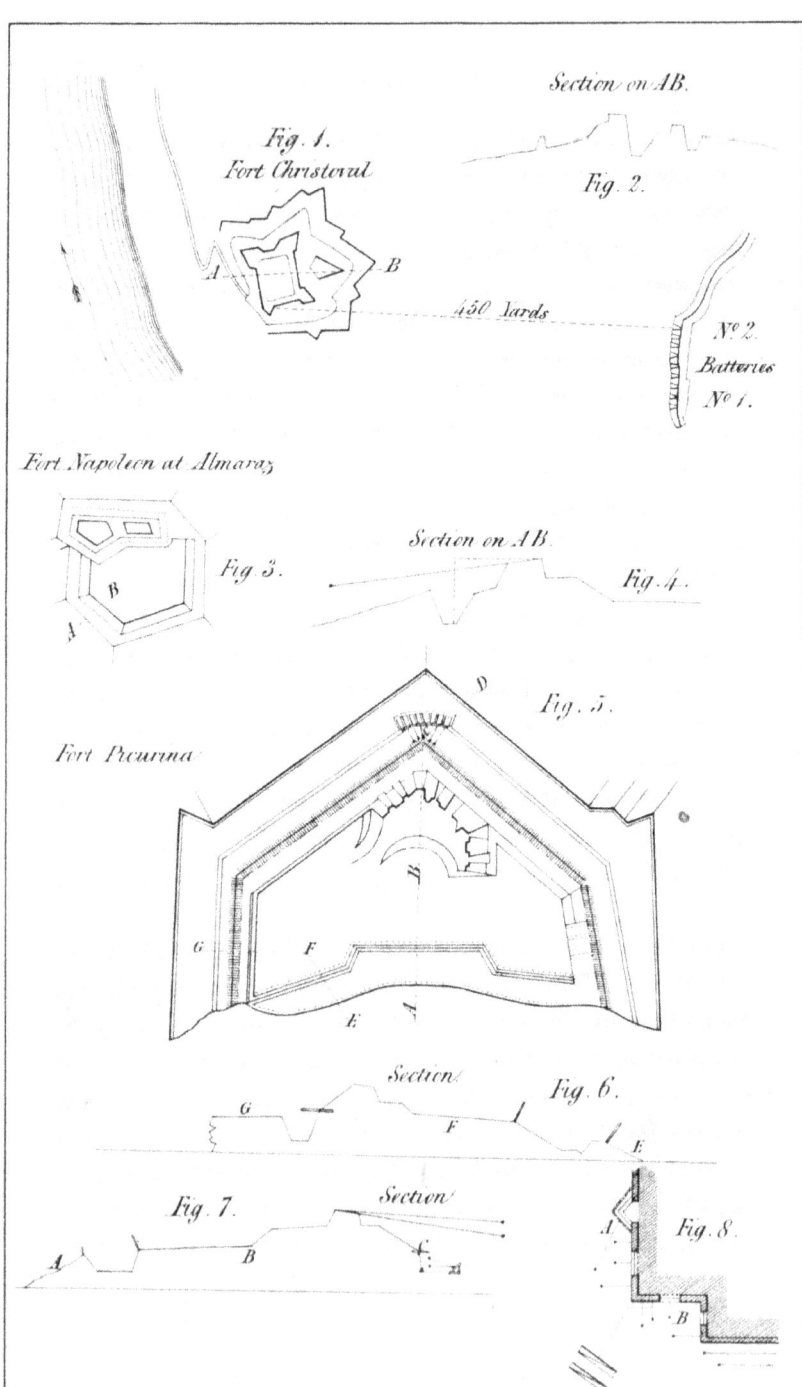

be no less instructive because they were failures. They are valuable as FACTS, exhibiting the terrible array which determined men have it in their power to develop for resisting an Assault, and the effect which the Means they do possess will produce; and likewise as Proofs that the most Heroic and Glorious efforts of the stoutest Arms and Hearts will not avail, unless they are seconded by ample Means for bringing them to bear. FIG. 1 will explain the nature of the Work, and its relative situation with the Parallel and Batteries, &c.

"*Assault of Christoval, on the night of the 6th of June.*

" The Breach in the Flank had been closely examined during the last night by Lieutenant Forster, who considered it to be then sufficiently practicable, and this day's firing having much improved its appearance, it was determined to assault it at dark; and the following dispositions for the Assault and Lodgment was issued with the sanction of General Houston.

"*Assault.*

" 1. The Detachment will consist of two companies of Grenadiers: one company will form the Assaulting party, and the other the Reserve.

" 2. The Assaulting party will be divided into two equal Detachments, the second following at 100 paces from the first; the advance of the Assaulting party will consist of an Officer and 25 men, who will, on the appointed signal, mount the Breach, and take immediate possession of the Gorge of the Work and its entrance.

"3. The Advance of the Assaulting party will be instantly followed by the remainder of the first Detachment, and after the whole have entered and cleared the Work, they will extend themselves from one side of the Fort to the other, where there they will remain covered as much as possible from the fire of the Castle.

"4. The Advance of the Assaulting party will be accompanied by an Officer of the Royal Engineers, with two Ladders, two Crowbars, and two Broad Axes; and 10 Ladders will be issued to the first Detachment as a Reserve, if found necessary.

"5. The Company forming the Reserve will place itself under the crest of the Glacis on the East face of the Work, and continue to divert the attention of the Garrison of the Fort by a brisk fire of Musketry.

"6. The whole of the Guard of the Trenches, or at least 300 men, will occupy the Ravine between Battery No. 2 and Fort Christoval, and will detach 50 men to the West side of the Fort, which Detachment, advancing as far as the Ditch, of the ruined Intrenchment between Fort Christoval and the Bridge head, will cut off that line of Communication with the Town.

"7. One Company, with one 6-pounder and a Howitzer, will advance along the Lower Road in the plain, East of the Height of Christoval, so as to interrupt any Communication by Boats across the Guadiana.

"8. It should be clearly understood that the Assaulting party *use only the Bayonet*, and that not a single Musket is fired on our part, unless the Enemy, by their fire, make our intentions evident. The company of Grenadiers to the East, and the 50 men detached from the Guard of the

Trenches on the West side of the Fort, will then endeavour to distract the attention of the Garrison, by rapid discharges of Musketry against the Parapets of the Work.

"*Lodgment.*

" One hundred Workmen to be employed in the Lodgment in Fort Christoval, to be divided into two Parties— 50 men in advance, and 50 men in Reserve: 25 of the first Detachment will carry Pickaxes, and 25 Shovels; the whole of the hundred men will carry a small Gabion: besides these there will be six Carpenters and six Miners, the Carpenters with three Saws and three Axes, the Miners with four Crowbars, besides Miners' Tools.

" After the Troops have gained possession of the Work, the Workmen will be employed in forming a covered Trench across the whole terreplein fronting the Castle, or in forming a sap along the Rampart, which, commencing in front of the Beach, shall continue from thence to the Demi-Bastion on the opposite side; thus forming a covered Communication from one side of the Fort to the other. Every exertion must be made to render the sap Cannon-proof before the morning, and to make the Breach practicable for the admission of the Artillery: the nature and direction of the sap must wholly depend on the form of the interior of the Work.

"*Execution of the Assault.*

" The Storming party consisted of 180 men. At midnight the advance of 25 men, conducted by Lieutenant Forster, Royal Engineers, moved forward from No. 1 Battery to the right Salient angle of the Ditch of the Fort, without being opposed by any great increase of fire from the Ramparts. The Palisades had been all destroyed by the fire of the Batteries, and the Counterscarp proved no Obstacle, being at that re-entering spot only 4 feet deep; the advance, therefore, readily descended into the Ditch in good order, but on attempting to mount the Breach it was found perfectly impracticable; the Garrison having moved the rubbish from the foot of it, during the period between dark and the attack, and the Scarp standing nearly 7 feet high. After making an unsuccessful attempt to get over this Obstacle, the advance were in the act of retiring, and would have come away with very little loss, had they not met the main body of the Storming party entering the Ditch. The Fort wa sevidently weakly manned, and the Garrison not having yet brought any very destructive Fire on the Assailants, the Officers considered the opportunity favourable for an attempt to force in by Escalade, and directed 12 ladders of 15 feet in length, which had been supplied with the view of aiding in mounting the Breach, to be applied against the Scarp wall. The Scarp being more than 20 feet high, the attempt proved abortive: other points of less height were sought, and the ladders were applied in vain to almost every Face and Flank of the Work. The Garrison showered upon the Assaulting party shells, hand grenades, stones, &c., in overwhelming quantities, for an hour, in which these impracticable attempts were persevered in. At 1 A.M. the residue of the party retired, having lost 12 killed and 90 wounded. Lieutenant Forster at the close of the combat received a shot through the body, of which he died."

This failure led to a second attempt being made on the night of the 9th of June with greater numbers, and such fresh arrangements as the experience which had been gained, dictated.

"*Disposition for the Second Assault.*

" 1. The Detachment for this service will consist of 400 men, and will be distributed in the following manner.

" 2. The Assaulting party will consist of 200 men, and will be divided into two Detachments of 100 men each : they will march from the rear of No. 1 and 2 Batteries together, having an interval between them of 50 paces. After arriving at the foot of the Heights of Christoval, the front Detachment will move up the hill in a direct line for the Breach, while the other Detachment marches directly for the Salient angle of the Work. A subaltern and 25 men will be detached from each party, and should always advance with an interval of about 30 paces between it and the remainder. After arriving at the Palisades, the Subaltern and 25 men of each party will proceed to the Assault with all possible dispatch, and as soon as the Advance shall have nearly entered the Work, the remainder of the 100 men of each party will follow, and take possesion of the Fort.

" 3. The Advance against the Breach will be accompanied by six ladders, the Advance against the Salient angle by 10 ladders.

" 4. During the Assault, a Detachment of 30 men will keep up a brisk fire of Musketry against the Parapets of the long Face of the Work between the Breach and the Salient angle.

"5. Seventy men will march along the Lower Road under the Height of Christoval, and will halt in the Lower ground, about 300 yards from the East end of the Height where it meets the River. At that point will be placed a Corporal and three men, to observe the passage of Boats across the River; and if any should attempt to cross over, the Detachment of 70 men will advance and prevent their landing, the object of this Detachment being to cut off the Communication across the Guadiana.

"6. One hundred men will move from the Campo-Maior road, nearly across the centre of the Parallel, and advance upon the West Front of the Work, keeping up a brisk fire of Musketry against the Parapets; and at the same time checking the Communication between the *Tête-de-Pont* and the Fort.

"7. The Guard of the Trenches will move forward to the hollow between No. 2 and Fort Christoval, and be ready to act as a Support as circumstances may require, detaching 30 men, who shall enter the advanced covered way, and keep up a fire against the parapets of the Work.

"8. Further to distract the attention of the Enemy, 50 men will be detached from the Guard of No. 4, about 300 yards to the Front, which shall keep up a Fire against the Parapets of the *Tête-de-Pont*. The Officer charged with this Service will take care to place his men (dividing them into two parties of 25 men each) as much as possible in the Flanks of the Work, so as not to be exposed to its Artillery.

"9. As soon as the interior is entered by the whole of the Storming party, the Detachment of 30 men which kept up the fire against the Parapets of the long face of the

Work will enter the Breach of the loop-holed Wall, and cut off the retreat of the Garrison.

"*Disposition for the Lodgment.*

"1. Lieutenant Hunt will follow in rear of the Advance of the Storming party, which moves forward to the Breach, and will be accompanied by 12 men carrying four Ladders, two Carpenters with Saws and Axes, and four Miners with Crowbars.

"2. As soon as the Advance have made good their entrance into the Work, Lieutenant Hunt, with the two Carpenters and four Miners, will follow the party and endeavour to overcome any Obstacle which may oppose their progress. He will reconnoitre the Work with all possible dispatch, and will search the Magazine, and destroy any lighted Match or Portfire he may meet with.

"3. As soon as all the Storming party have entered the Fort, and we have completely established ourselves, Captain Ross will advance with the Working party, which will be employed in the following manner.

"4. The Working party will be divided into two Detachments of 50 men each: 25 of the first Detachment will carry Pickaxes; and 25, Shovels. The whole of the 100 men will carry a small Gabion; and Captain Ross will also be accompanied by 12 men of the Brigades now attached to the Park.

"*Execution of the Assault.*

"The Assaulting Party paraded in the ravine behind Batteries Nos. 1 and 2, immediately that it became sufficiently dark for concealment, and every precaution of firing on the Breach was adopted to prevent a recurrence of its being cleared, and 16 ladders, from 25 to 30 feet long, were provided to aid the Assault by an Escalade; but circumstances had changed since the former attack. The French were then unprepared, and had only 75 men in the Fort: this evening they were on the alert, and had an ample Garrison in it, who, elated by recent success, received the Assailants with cheers and invitations to approach. The Advance moved forward at 9 P.M. under a most rapid fire of musketry from all the parapets of the Work, which opened upon them the moment they quitted the shelter of the Batteries. The first division of the Assaulting Party followed at the prescribed distance, with the utmost regularity, notwithstanding the heavy fire to which they were exposed and dsecended into the Ditch. Lieutenant Hunt, of the Engineers, conducting this division, was killed on the Glacis. Major M'Geachy, the Officer in command, immediately afterwards fell, and the next in seniority and many men were at the same moment disabled. The remainder, however, followed the advance towards the Breach; but an immense number of Shells and Combustibles rolled upon them from the Parapets of the Fort, added to the cool bravery displayed by the Defenders, checked their efforts and saved the Breach.

"The second Detachment of 100 men advanced with the same steadiness as the first, and descended into the Ditch without much loss. They then applied the Ladders to the Scarp, and succeeded in rearing most of them. The men ascended the Ladders with great readiness, but every one who succeeded in reaching the Parapet was instantly bayoneted down, and the Garrison after a little while mounted on the Parapet upset the Ladders. At this time the two Assaulting Columns were completely mixed together, and united in many strenuous endeavours to replace the Ladders at various points of the Fronts; but the enormous quantity of large Shells, Hand Grenades, bags of Powder and Combustibles, which the Garrison threw into the Ditch, rendered their perseverance and gallantry unavailing; and after braving destruction till 10 P.M., and having 40 men killed and 100 wounded, the remainder of the Assaulting Party was ordered to retire."

We have now the advantage of the OPINION and OBSERVATIONS of this distinguished Author on the two Operations.

"A practicable Breach having been formed in Fort Christoval at the point selected, it only required the aid of a co-operating Fire on the Defences, with a body of Sappers, and the necessary Fascines and Gabions, to have rendered the reduction of the Work certain; for in the period between the 30th May, the night of breaking ground, and the 6th of June, the night of the Assault, there was abundant time to have carried a Sap forward to the Glacis, and to have established such a *close Front of Musketry Fire* as should have prevented the Garrison from clearing the Breach, or showing themselves above the Parapets during the Attack. Then as the Troops would have been able to advance under cover to the Assault, it might have been made in Daylight, and with a certainty of success.

"The most critical examination of the Operations of this Siege* will not allow of blame for its failure being

---

* Of Badajos.

thrown on any one. From the General to the Soldier each did his duty, nor should want of success discredit the original Project. It must be admitted that there was a judicious application of all the Means that could be collected for the reduction of Christoval. On trial *those Means proved insufficient;* many of the causes of their insufficiency could not have been foreseen, and others if foreseen, could not have been remedied; all that skill and bravery could effect, was done."

Calculations of the means required for carrying on a Siege with vigour, and ensuring the reduction of a Fortress in the shortest time and with the least loss, appears in PART III., on Siege Duties. A comparison of these calculations with the actual force employed at the Sieges in the Peninsula, will show under what serious disadvantages they were undertaken, and how much is therefore due to the unshaken gallantry and perseverance of the Troops.

CHAP. III.—SURMOUNTING OBSTACLES.

12. In the attack of Military Posts, especially such as are of minor importance, Infantry are frequently thrown entirely upon their own resources, for forcing a passage through whatever Obstructions they may fall in with, before they close with their Adversaries. They may have no Guns or Howitzers for tearing up and destroying Stockades, Abattis, Palisading, Chevaux de Frise, &c., and have only to trust to their own exertions for getting to the *right side* of them. The nature of the Obstructions which are usually employed for adding strength to fortified Posts, are detailed in CHAP. V., PART I., and the means to be adopted for surmounting them, will now be briefly adverted to.

How to Deal with an Abattis.

13. An Abattis is probably the first Obstacle a Column will fall in with, and an awkward customer it is, if it has been properly managed, and that the Materials have been of sufficient size and weight. In an Attack by Surprise an endeavour should be made to get round the Flank of it, and if that " won't do," the men must try and crawl through it in the best manner they can, avoiding any noise, and forming again as they succeed; should they be caught at this proceeding, it must be "bock again" with the leading files.

14. If the Attack is by Open Force, and the Abattis should prove a puzzler, there is no harm in making the attempt to set it on fire. A few resolute fellows carrying small Faggots, which for the sake of a good "flare up" may as well have been previously dipped in pitch, and each

man provided with a lighted "portfire" if it is daytime; or if they can approach unseen by night, with some other means of setting fire to them,—must rush up from some neighbouring place of concealment, covered by a smart fire of Musketry, and throwing in their lighted faggots, all will soon be in a blaze. When that has subsided, and there is no fear of the men's pouches being exploded, the Breach will be practicable without waiting for the hot cinders to cool, for they will only prove stimulants to exertion, and will make the people "vivacious." This little conflagration would go on under the protection of a Party, near enough to prevent any attempt on the part of the Defenders to extinguish it. If, however, an Abattis is formed of small materials, or that sufficient precautions have not been taken to secure it in its place; that is, if it is *a bad one*, it will be a waste of time to submit to the delay of burning it. In such a case, a Party rushing up with ropes, may tie them to some principal Trees; or a big Hook, fixed to a rope or pole, such as the Worshipful Companies of Firemen have for their work, may be used, and a Tree or two may by these means, be dragged forcibly out of the Line;—or some handy fellows with good tools may partially open it, by cutting away a few of the small branches, so as to let men get through at "Open Order." A little impudence will go a long way sometimes; and in cases of necessity, putting a a good face on a dangerous enterprise, is the best handmaid to success.

How to Macadamise other Impediments.

15. If the Obstructions outside a Post consist of Military Pits, Stakes, or the Stumps of Trees, &c., they may be passed at "Open order" if they cannot be avoided, and

SURMOUNTING OBSTACLES.

the Columns be re-formed as soon as possible. Small Ditches may be filled up with faggots or bundles of hay; Chevaux de Frise may be displaced by main force, with a rope, and a good pull altogether; or they may be cut up or blown to pieces with a bag of powder; Palisades or fraises in a ditch may be got rid of in a similar manner; or if a party is provided with Ladders or Planks, and the Ditches are narrow, these last Obstructions will frequently offer facilities for constructing temporary Bridges for passing over them. Stockade work or Palisading may be Escaladed with Ladders brought up in a line under the protection of a Firing Party, and carried by two or four men, according to their length. The Ladders would be planted as close together as they conveniently could be, and the Assailants would mount them, on as extended a Front as their numbers permitted; or a Stockade may be breached by the explosion of a bag of powder, &c. By some such means as these, applied with boldness and decision, in a common sense sort of way, Troops assisted by Workmen would be a match for any of the ordinary Obstructions which might oppose their advance, whether the Attack were made by Night or by Day, by Surprise or by Open Force.

If none of these means should be exactly at hand or applicable, something or other that would answer the purpose would doubtless suggest itself; a man only requires to be thrown violently on his own resources and it will strike fire out of him, if at other times he exhibits no more signs of life than a bit of Flint or a Zoophyte.

CHAP. IV.—OF ATTACKS BY SURPRISE.

16. A Post is said to be *Surprised*, when an Enemy either gets into it, or close up to it,—by making a false or forced march, information of which has been concealed from the Defenders, either by their own bad look out, or their Opponents having been favoured by fog or darkness, &c.; or it may be, that they have succeeded in quietly cutting off some Advanced Post, which would have given the alarm.

17. When ably planned and carried into execution, a Surprise is the best kind of Attack that can be made; there is less *Exposure* beforehand, and from being unexpected, there is, from the nature of things, more confusion among the Defenders, and therefore less *Resistance* afterwards. The result also is generally more decisive, and smaller numbers can act with far greater effect against a Superior Force, than can be hoped for in an Open Attack. It is only however when an Adversary fails in his precautionary measures that success can be confidently anticipated, even from the best formed scheme of Surprise; and then, without precise information as to the nature of the Defences,— the Strength of the Defenders, and their measures of Security,—without ascertaining the *degree* of caution and punctuality, with which the Duties are performed, any attempt at a Surprise would most probably fail.

18. Neglect in the *External* precautions of Security, such as a faulty disposition of the outlying Picquets and Videttes—the omission of Patrolling, &c. *admits* of a Sur-

prise; and an absence of judicious *Internal* arrangements will *facilitate* it. The first, will consist in placing but few Picquets, and those at too great a distance from each other, and too far to the Front, so that the Chain becomes unconnected, and that the communication between them is not properly preserved; or in falling into an opposite error, of placing them so near to a Post as that they do not secure sufficient notice of the presence of a Hostile Force, to enable the Defenders to stand to their arms;—or it may be traced to a slovenly manner of carrying on the Outpost Duty generally. The second, will depend upon the degree of Discipline and Readiness prevailing among the Troops generally, and the Dispositions that may have been made for applying their services in the most effective manner, and in the shortest possible time, &c. The following are likewise circumstances that will favour this mode of proceeding.

19. When there is a Wood or Ravine within a moderate distance of a Post;—when you have the the power of secretly assembling a Force equal to the undertaking, which was before dispersed with a different object;—when the Defenders think themselves in security, either from your distance or circumstances, and are therefore less on their guard and less vigilant;—if the Post is not quite complete in the Works designed for its Defence,—if the Troops are raw, and their Chief not much better;—or if, from being deemed inaccessible when that fact is fabulous, any part is not so well guarded as others; these are all very tempting circumstances to try one's luck at a Surprise.

20. Secrecy is the soul of a Surprise; and as a secret is liable to "fructify" when in the hands of many, the less

D

that is said about any intention of beating up a neighbour's quarters the better. Your Enemies must of course be deceived, or kept in ignorance, and until the moment when their exertions are required, it would be quite as well for your Friends to be so too. The requisite preparations, therefore, in collecting Ladders, Tools, &c., should be shielded under cover of being for some other distinct operation, and plausible excuses given forth to allay suspicions as they arise.

21. Among other considerations, it will have to be decided beforehand whether the Post is to be held and defended should it be taken, or whether it is to be destroyed or abandoned. In the former case, a temporary supply of Provisions and Ammunition should be thought of; in the latter, the Attack and Retreat only have to be provided for.

22. Winter is the most favourable time of the year for attempting a Surprise. Sentries are not usually so much on the alert in cold weather, and the long Nights and the Storms and Fogs, which prevail at that season, are all "accessaries before the fact." A night when the moon sets just before you want to begin the Attack is advantageous, as the previous movements will have all the benefit of the light, and the succeeding darkness may serve an equally good purpose; but while it is on the tapis, it may not be amiss to bestow a little further considerations on the subject of *Time*, for whether it be a Joke or an Attack, it is half the battle to time it well.

23. It is generally admitted that the peep of day is, under most circumstances, very favourable for making an Open Attack, when there is not light enough to betray the Advance or any of the preparatory movements, and the

Assailants have the advantage of daylight immediately after to profit by success in securing all the advantages they may have gained. But an Enemy knows this as well as anybody else, and the whole disposable Force of an Army or Garrison, is generally under arms at that time, and probably more on the "look out for squalls" than at any other hour of the twenty-four. This, therefore, is not the best time to catch them napping, and it would appear, that getting up a little earlier, or sitting up a little later than one's adversary, would afford a better opportunity. As to Time therefore, soon after midnight would probably be the hour when snoring would be loudest; and if it could be made to square with the object in view, which may vary with circumstances, it would probably be as favourable a time for the attempt as any other: for example, if the Post were at no great distance, and the intention was to destroy and then abandon it, before succour could arrive, a better hour than midnight could not be selected, as it would afford the opportunity of accomplishing the object, and making good the Retreat before daylight. But if the Post were to be held afterwards, the dawn of day immediately after the Assault, would enable a Party to make better arrangements for defending itself, and later attack would therefore be preferable.

24. From these considerations it will appear that a Surprise, whether early or late, generally entails a Night Attack, and it is scarcely necessary to say that the greatest precautions, and the very best Arrangements, are required for carrying it into effect; nor can success be reasonably looked for, without them. The worst of going to work in the dark is, that unless the point to be attacked is of a nature not to be mistaken, it is ten to one the attempt to

OF ATTACKS BY SURPRISE.

identify what is doubtful will disclose all. Nothing can be worse than having to poke about, especially if you don't want to be found out, which is rather an essential in a Surprise. Again, when you have forced an entrance, we will say into a Village, unless you are perfectly acquainted with the interior, and familiar with every object that presents itself, there are other and great disadvantages to contend against. The Local knowledge of the Defenders is all in their favour: the offensive cannot be continued with vigour, and nothing is gained in furtherance of your object by standing still: Dangers are magnified in the dark, especially when men are not excited; and as a resolute Enemy will know exactly where to strike the blow, and you can neither see from whence it comes, nor estimate its force, till you feel its effect, it may become necessary to assume a Defensive attitude, and this under the circumstances may lead to a reversal of your previous success. If there is work to do with the shovel and pickaxe, such as effecting a Lodgment for establishing yourself on the ground that has been gained, or for other purposes, the darkness is favourable for the execution of it; but this does not affect the present question. Under any circumstances, however, the value of the Local knowledge which is conspicuous among the useful items adverted to in No. 1, will be apparent, and, with other hints which have been thrown out, will serve to create a suspicion that there is something for a Commander to think of, before he makes up his mind to commit himself in action.*

---

* Surprises in the open day can seldom be successfully undertaken, except in Mountainous Countries, intersected by Ravines and Hollow Roads, &c.

OF ATTACKS BY SURPRISE. 37

25. The number of men for an Attack ought under most circumstances to be superior to the force of the Defenders, which it must not be forgotten have the vantage ground; but in a well-conceived and vigorously executed Surprise, very inferior numbers profiting by the confusion and astonishment, which are inseparable from an unexpected Attack, have done "*impossible things,*" and doubtless can do so again; which it is as well to remember when any similar opportunity should happen on service. Generally, however, Numbers are one principal ingredient in success, and therefore the means for the Attack should be adequate to the object, taken in all its bearings. A very inferior Force may possibly make good their footing, against all opposition at any certain point, but the question may be, can they maintain it?

26. This question arises with a greater or less demand for an answer in the affirmative, according to circumstances. For example, a modest Commander may prescribe limits to his ambition, and merely wish to set fire to a Post, a Village, or Dockyard, or to blow up a Magazine, or some other equally inviting subject, and then peaceably to retire without any desire further to trespass on the time or attention of his Opponents. A few minutes' possession of a certain spot might suffice for the accomplishment of any of these purposes, and it might be that a very few men would be sufficient to force an entrance and effect them. In a well-concerted Surprise, a small Force might possibly be brought almost within arm's length of the desired object without discovery, and when a rush was made for securing it, there might be all the routine of sounding the "Alarm and Assembly," of turning out Guards,

and probably some marching and counter-marching to perform, before the nature of the Attack, or even the point or points where it was made, were clearly comprehended by any large body of the Defenders; and before they had rubbed their eyes, and made their Dispositions for repelling it, the deed might be done, and the actors be on their way home again. Here it would appear, that to lay down the law of *Disproportion*, that may reign between the contending parties, might be to throw a " wet blanket" on some daring deed, yet in the womb of time, the contemplation of which might be affected by any preconceived notions on a subject which cannot well be defined. If a man to a sound head unites a stout heart, and though last not least—a good stomach, (for *that* has its influence upon nerves they say,) and that he sees quite clearly what he has to do, and how it is to be done; moreover, if he has people with him that he can depend upon, there is scarcely any thing *impossible*, where physical impossibilities do not intervene; we might safely say to such an one, "Go along, Mister, with a face of cruelty, and do it audacious!"

27. If, however, the Post which is attacked, is to be held afterwards, "*c'est une autre chose;*" Defenders have an unpleasant way of sometimes recovering from a first panic, and then the preponderance of Force should be on the right side, or "the tables may be turned." There have been instances, however, quite within the memory of the present generation, of a very inferior Force surrounding a respectable Work strongly garrisoned,—carrying it by Assault in the night, and making the Defenders lay down their arms before daylight told any tales as to the disparity of numbers.

OF ATTACKS BY SURPRISE. 39

The success of such Enterprises, as these which have for their object to effect what greater numbers ought to be employed about, depends entirely on the advantages resulting to them from a complete Surprise, and coming upon an Enemy, when he is quite unprepared: in fact, if this is not done, the attempt ought to be abandoned at once.

28. The execution of an Attack of this nature is rather a delicate affair, for if by any means the suspicions of a vigilant Adversary have been awakened, he will have made such Dispositions as might cause the Surprise to be felt on the *wrong* side. If, therefore, there should be the least cause for believing that an Enemy is playing tricks, every possible precaution should be taken for ascertaining the truth before getting into a mess, which it might be difficult to get out of. The Main Body should be halted at a greater distance than it is likely an Ambuscade would be sent, and the whole ground in the front should be "*felt*," with the utmost caution by Patrols, who if not stopped by Outlying Picquets or Videttes, &c., should creep close up to the place, and do a little "eaves-dropping," in listening to everything that is going on. If on their report it should be decided to move on, it would still be prudent to do so with all circumspection, having an Advanced Guard composed of men who know what they are about, and Parties with the same view to protection on either Flank. If, on the contrary, there were good reason to believe that the Enterprise was no secret, and that everything was in readiness to give you a warm reception, it would depend upon circumstances whether "prudence," would not be "the better part of valour." These observations of course only apply to a Force quite inadequate to any open attempt;

but with a proportionate Force, should there be a failure in the design of surprising a Post, the probability of which would have been foreseen and provided for, it would only be necessary, under such circumstances, to throw off the mask, proclaim yourself an open Enemy, and fight it out, which all your previous arrangements would enable you to do without difficulty.

29. The whole Force employed, whatever it may be, should be divided for fulfilling specific objects. Several Columns of Attack may have to be formed; some for false, others for real Attacks—each to be closely followed by its Support, No. 6: there should also be a certain Force posted in Reserve for covering a Retreat, in case of failure; another probably for guarding particular points, in order that should your designs have been anticipated, you may not be suprised in your turn by an attack in flank or rear. Men with Axes, Sledge-hammers, Crow-bars, &c., for forcing Barricades, or cutting away Obstacles, and a few bags of Powder with Fuses attached, for bursting open Gates, (No. 37,) would be useful. The Troops employed on these little Enterprises should be picked Men: those who are weak, and those troubled with coughs, should be drafted off and left at home; the *former* would not be in a condition for work, and the *latter* would most likely betray your arrival at the moment it was of the utmost importance to conceal it; Horses, for the same reason, should be left at a distance. Guides, if they can be depended on, will be necessary in sufficient numbers to allow two or three to accompany each party, but *personal* knowledge in the Assailants or their Leaders, is a better thing, and more conducive to success.

30. Whatever may be the Time or Disposition that is decided upon, the march must be so ordered as that the Column or Columns shall arive at some point in the immediate neighbourhood, perhaps a mile, or a mile and a half distant, an hour or more before they will be wanted, so that the last orders may be given, and the final arrangements be made, for there is generally a parting word to say on these occasions. This will not be a bad opportunity either, after a long march, for the men to strengthen their hearts by a mouthful of bread and cheese, if their haversacks afford it, for it may be some time before they will have leisure to breakfast. This arrangement for the marchpresupposes that all the requisite information respecting the situation of the Picquets,—the mode of Patrolling,—and the general *external* precautions for guarding a Post have been obtained, so that a Commander knows what he is about, and can put his different Detachments in movement for the several points he intends to attack. But if this information has still to be sought, in consequence of the Enemy's Picquets being posted differently every night, or other causes, the Troops must either be brought up earlier, and wait till these points are determined; or a Patrolling Party must precede them, so as to get there at dusk, and have it all ready. In the former case, arriving at the halting place by such Roads as afford the best means of concealment, some steady and intelligent men should be detached to patrole to the front; first to ascertain if possible the situation of any Picquets which might have been posted wide apart, and then to find out the order in which the Videttes were placed,—the mode of Patrolling between them,—and any further information that could be obtained.

The success of the Enterprise depends upon the chance of introducing the whole Force unperceived within the chain of Picquets. The state of the weather will materially facilitate this preliminary step, and when it has been accomplished, the advance should be continued until the Columns are discovered by the Sentries of the Post, when a general rush would be made, and the more impetuous the Attack, the more favourable for the object, of following up the *Surprise* by an easy *Conquest*.

DISTRIBUTION OF THE ASSAILANTS, &c.

31. A multiplicity of considerations will influence the distribution of the Assailants, so that it is hopeless to lay down any rule of general application; but we might say on a broad principle, that it would not be prudent to divide a small Force too much in attempting false Attacks, and that therefore, from one-half to two-thirds of it might be formed for the Assault, keeping the remainder in Reserve for Covering the Retreat, and acting according to circumstances; or were the Force considerable, and the Post to be attacked of corresponding extent, such as an Intrenched Village, perhaps one-third of the numbers might be formed for the Principal Attack, another third be divided for two false Attacks, and the remainder be left in reserve for the purposes before stated. In the former case, as a minimum, the Assailants should be at least equal in numbers to the Defenders; and in the latter, as the Force is more divided, there should be a proportionate increase; that is to say, the numbers engaged in the three Attacks should be stronger than the Garrison. A part of the Force engaged in the false Attacks, or a portion of the Reserve, should be

placed not very far from the Entrances to the Post that are nearest to the point where the real Attack is going on. These may be Streets, Roads, or Gateways, &c., and they should be watched, that advantage may be taken of their being turned or opened; some Workmen, who are "good at need" for breaking open Barricades, being held in readiness to accompany the Party.

32. When all these particulars had been arranged, and that the Officers or Non-commissioned Officers commanding the several Parties had been made clearly to understand their orders, and the specific objects confided to them;— when the conduct they should observe under every emergency, both during the Attack, and in the event of success or failure, had been explained; when the precise moment on which the Attacks should take place was perfectly understood, and that some conventional signal, countersign or badge, had been established by which men could recognise each other in the dark, the Columns would be in readiness to move on. The advance would be made in silence, and without haste; the Columns dividing when they got near the place, and marching by the best route to their points, preceded by a few steady Soldiers as an Advanced Guard, who would be on the look out to secure any Patroles or Videttes they might fall in with, so as to prevent their giving the alarm.

Of the Attack.

33. If the object of a Column were to assault a Field Work, which has usually a Ditch bounded by slopes of Earth, the Advance of the Storming Party would silently slide down into the bottom of it, and if there were no

Obstacles, such as Palisades, &c., and that the slopes admitted of their scrambling up, they would form in the bottom of the Ditch, in Subdivisions, or Sections, as might be ordered, and endeavour to go up together without straggling; the remainder of the Party following them as closely as possible; the Support being halted at the edge of the Ditch, ready to fire or advance, and the Reserve being posted further off.

34. If there were unforeseen Obstacles, which could not be got over or removed without the noise of Workmen, the secrecy of the operation would be nearly over, and it would be time to awaken the *astonishment* of the Garrison. A few preparations being made, such as the Storming Party lying down opposite the spot, and the Support or a Firing Party, on either Flank ready to keep people off the top of the Parapet, the Workmen would glide into the Ditch, and first distributing themselves judiciously, and finding what was to be done, and the best way of doing it, they would commence work together, and regardless of any thing that might happen, would lay about them, till they had accomplished their task; when the Assault would immediately be given, and the endeavour would be made to Charge in column, through whatever Force was formed for the defence of the Parapet: when this was accomplished, a halt would be made, to reform for further Operations in following up the advantage gained.

35. After Troops once move forward to the Assault, the Bayonet should be called upon to do all the work; very little is gained by the Leading Files firing down upon the Defenders from the top of the Parapet, especially in the dark, or the grey of the morning. It only has a tendency

to check their speed, at the moment it is of some use to them. The Assailants are at that time exposed and perfectly visible against the sky, when the Defenders, however near, could not be seen, and after the first man has jumped down within a Work, his comrades must of necessity cease firing; therefore anything that would be gained by permitting its use, would be more than outweighed by the inconveniences that would be entailed. It is usual therefore to make use of the Bayonet only on these occasions.

36. If a Wall or any other Obstacle of a moderate height had to be scaled, the Ladders would be carried by the Advanced Party, who would plant them side by side, and after its being ascertained that all were properly in their places, the Troops would advance up them in the most compact order, and jumping down inside, would form again and move forward, as soon as circumstances permitted. Stockade work might be scaled in the same way.

Blowing open Barriers, &c.

37. In the Attack of Gateways or Houses, if secrecy is preserved till you get close to them, it is as much as can be expected. In order to force the Barriers or Doors, the most effectual agent is a Bag of Gunpowder. A bag containing from 20 to 30 or 40 lbs, according to the expected strength of the Obstacle, and furnished with a Fuse for firing it, and a Loop to hang it by, can be easily nailed or hooked up against a pair of Gates, or fastened to a barricaded Door. If it can be done without previous discovery so much the better, and for effecting this, a gimlet will be found a very useful, quiet operator. When fixed, the Fuse is lighted, and the man retires a little. The Party for

forcing an entrance may be drawn up within 15 or 20 yards, and a few expert men with Axes and Sledge-hammers may be with them. The Explosion will most probably do all that is required, and the ruins, if any remain to impede the advance, will quickly be got rid of by the Workmen. If all this has been done in secret, it will be a great object to take advantage of the bustle and confusion that will ensue by making a vigorous Attack. If, however, the secrecy of the Operation is at an end before the Bag is fixed, and that this has to be effected by open violence, in spite of what may be attempted to prevent it, the best proceeding is for a strong Firing Party to rush up, and throwing themselves under any Cover that might offer, to reply to, and endeavour to subdue, the Fire that defends the point to be attacked, and when that slackened, the men with the Bag of Powder would make a run of it,—Fix—Light—and " be off."

SECURING POSSESSION OF A POST AFTER A SURPRISE.

38. In the Attack of a Village, or even of a smaller Post, the moment an entry is is made, a portion of the Force should be detached, to endeavour to communicate with the other Attacks, if there were any; and leaving a Party in reserve at the point where they came in, they should secretly march, if the alarm had not been given, to secure the Guards and principal Avenues into the Village. By thus gaining possession of the Barricades or Gates they would be enabled to open a communication, by which a portion of the Reserve, which should have been previously held in readiness, might enter. If they were discovered, and that the Garrison were assembling to oppose them, the same

measures would be of advantage, and no time should be lost in also making a furious attack on the Main Body, wherever it might be forming, taking care, during the advance, to secure the means of an orderly Retreat. The value of *Local knowledge,* indeed its absolute necessity, is again apparent, for how could any of these steps be taken with the promptness befitting the occasion, if this were wanting?

In the case of an Intrenched Village, the Keep should be looked up, and might be attacked in the mode pointed out in CHAP. VIII.; and if there were Barracks, Huts, or a Camp, immediate measures would be taken to march there, and profit by the confusion. The principle on which such movements would be made, however, fall, more or less, within the scope of the ordinary Instruction in the Field, and will not therefore be further dwelt upon.

CHAP. V.—OF ATTACKS BY OPEN FORCE.

39. An Attack by Open Force is imposed, when something like the converse of all the circumstances that would favour an Attack by Surprise exists;—such as the Ground outside a Post affording no Cover for approaching it,—or when a Post is so well and so vigilantly guarded, that the Defenders are "not to be done,"—or it becomes a measure of necessity when a Force is driven "to take the Bull by the Horns," from having no choice left between an Attack, or a Retreat, as might happen in a General Action; or an Attack of this nature may be undertaken with confidence when the Works are weak or unfinished, and where there are facilities for Enfilading its principal lines with Artillery;— or when a Commander is known to have a "screw loose" in his nerves, or his powers of arrangement, &c.

40. Most of the information required for judiciously planning an Attack by Surprise, (CHAP. IV.,) will be also of essential service, when an Attack by Open Force is contemplated; in either case it is equally of importance that a knowledge of the Locale should be previously obtained, and that the Obstacles to be overcome should be carefully estimated, and compared with the means proposed for surmounting them, before Troops are committed in the Attempt; something must of necessity be left to chance and good fortune, but not too much. If a choice exists as to Time, the most favourable hour for making such an Attack must be determined in reference to some of the *pros* and *cons* in No. 23, as far as they might be applicable.—Should it so

OF ATTACKS BY OPEN FORCE. 49

happen that circumstances permitted a Force to evade any previous exposure, by attacking in the night, or before daylight, so much the better; but if the Attack is made in the open day, and there is neither natural nor artificial *cover* to favour the Enterprise, the strongest and most energetic measures should be adopted to control or subdue the Fire, that would be poured in upon an advancing Column; which is the worst treatment it has to endure, because it is in no condition for making a reply " *in kind.*" When the leading Files get within arm's-length of the Defenders, an exchange of blows may take place, but not before; hence the advantage of a " Cloud of Light Troops," as our Old Friend calls them, or of a strong Firing Party, for the specific purpose of protecting Columns engaged in the attack of works of whatever description they may be.

41. Though there is a great difference in the two modes of Attack under discussion, because in one, it is assumed that an Enemy is half asleep, and in the other, that he is on the alert, and that all the means in his power will be developed to oppose it, yet in their *Principles they are the same;* and as a notion of these principles, and of further details may perhaps have been obtained from the preceding Chapter in which they are adverted to, a repetition of them would be superfluous.

42. The points requiring attention and the dispositions to be made after a successful Assault, have also been glanced at in No. 38, and equally apply to the more open mode of Attack under consideration. But as an Enemy will be better prepared for making Resistance, the measures will require to be of a more decided character, and no time should be lost in following up the advantage of a first success. A

Reserve would be left at the point where the entry was effected, and according to circumstances strong Detachments would be sent off to the right and left, to follow the Enemy, and sweep the interior of the defences; leaving Guards at every entrance of a street, road, or alley, by which they might be cut off. The Gates and principal avenues opening towards the side attacked would be seized, and access given to Troops from the Reserve which should be held in readiness to enter, and an impetuous Attack would be made on the Main Body as soon as a sufficient Force was assembled. If there were a Keep, the the attack should threaten the Communication with their stronghold, and if circumstances permitted, a rush should be made to cut off their Retreat to it, or to *intrude*, by joining the Party and going in with them: we do not say much about being *beat*, because with skilful dispositions, adequate means, and Columns that will "go ahead," there is little reason to anticipate such a disaster. In any case, however, in which unexpected failure attended a first Assault, (and accidents will sometimes happen,) the Troops would fall back on the Reserve in good order, and as soon as fresh dispositions could be made, the Assault should be given again, with any additional force, or precautions, which experience might have shown to be necessary.

CHAP. VI.—ATTACK OF AN INTRENCHED VILLAGE.

43. A certain Character in some Comedy or other, when applied to for his opinion of "things in general," or on any subject "in particular," calls to a Yorkshire Friend of his, who is a shrewd fellow, to help him,—" York, you're wanted," says he; and in like manner it would be throwing away a chance, did not we, in dipping into a fresh subject appeal, as heretofore, to our Old Friend, to give us a sketch by way of a Frontispiece. He is as cheerful and full of fight as ever: speaking of the " Reconnoissance" he says, " When you are charged with the Attack of an Intrenched Village, go under the escort of a few of your best men, telescope in hand, and in the same uniform; go and explore all the environs for yourself, and make a rough sketch and memorandum of what you observe. Do you see that height from which you can enfilade the main Street of the Village from one end to the other?—Put one of your principal Batteries there.—That little wood now occupied by the Enemy will be capital ground for your Skirmishers up to the very gates of the place; that Road which is cut through in several places will be easily repaired;—that little undulation of the ground;—Stop! which do you mean? Oh! your unpractised eye cannot see it, but there it is, and an excellent situation you will find it for assembling your Columns of Assault. There; now you can see all the new Works the enemy has executed;—you may reckon up his Forces if you look sharp: he is still at work

ATTACK OF AN INTRENCHED VILLAGE.

at that place where you see the fresh earth, and that great building is his keep: where you see that loop-holed Wall, must be a weakish place; but the approach is difficult on account of that Redoubt. Never mind! make a Battery to silence it. By the bye, that Farm-house yonder, on the outside, is occupied in force; you must get possession of that first, or you'll be in a scrape. If you could but get a little nearer, so as to see all, it would be better, but it cannot be helped, and what you do not discover to day, your Light Troops, will find out for you to-morrow. Now go back and make your dispositions for the Attack;—give your orders, and afterwards take a walk among the Soldiers at their Bivouacs: go up to their fires and address yourself in a friendly manner to them,—tell them what a famous day you'll have to-morrow. Your air of confidence and your little sallies—spiced up here and there with a touch of military glory, will persuade the most timid that there is a very easy affair before them, and will fortify the courage of all."

After this, he waxes warm on the subject of the Attack, and delivers himself to the following effect:—" Before day-break the Troops have breakfasted, already the Advanced Guard is under arms, and on the move, so as to arrive at the first dawn, at the advanced posts of the Enemy. The Columns form and follow them; and last of all comes the Artillery. Objects begin to be just discernable and the advanced Detachments recognise the Posts which are to be attacked. They approach for a time unperceived, but at length,—Bang!! a Round Shot comes right among them, a rattling fire of Musketry succeeds, and their arrival is announced. Then begins the game of the Light Troops;

and the Sun rises to witness all the Out-posts in the power of the Assailants! Meanwhile the Artillery trot up, take their position, and open a tremendous fire, in reply to that of the Enemy, which they soon reduce to silence, and then they thunder away against the walls :—numberless breaches appear; the shot bounds along the Streets, and compel the Defenders to conceal themselves behind the houses or in their Redoubt; the shells bursting in all parts leave them no repose. 'Go along you Cripples!' cries an unfeeling Wag! Several Houses take Fire, and a horrible Explosion, which for a length of time covers the Village with a dense mass of smoke, bears witness to the interminable disasters of the Enemy. The Voltiguers spring forward and surround the Village on all sides; the Guns cease firing; the Troops of the Line prepare to march; the Enemy is harassed by this cloud of Skirmishers gradually closing in upon them, the boldest of whom are at the very Breach. The Sappers who accompany them level the hedges, and burst open the gates; some of them penetrate, others follow; and the uninterrupted chain which they instinctively form, traces the route which conducts to Glory. 'The plot thickens;' now sounds the Signal of Attack: the Columns issue from the hollows which have hitherto concealed them ; they cross the space which separates them from their Enemies at 'best pace,' and arrive to the timely support of the Light Troops who are paying the price of their eagerness, and are now pouring out of the breaches hotly pressed by the Defenders. The game's alive ! The heads of the Columns present themselves before the principal avenues; they upset the Barricades, scale the Parapets, and hew for themselves new roads ; whilst the Light Troops enter by other openings, charge the hedges, jump the Walls; and by this irresistible Storm, the Enemy is driven into his strongholds. The exterior Defences being overcome, the Troops rally, and forming in such order of battle as localities may dictate, take further steps for surrounding and exterminating their Adversaries. Up comes the Artillery at a gallop. The Church must be assaulted! there they have taken refuge! 'Action to the Front' is the word, and shot without mercy or number are poured in upon this principal defensive Post. By Jupiter! out they go by the back door, and make play across the Plain!— they run for their lives, but it won't do! The Cavalry are at their heels,—and cut them up in the open. Still a Redoubt holds out which has never ceased firing during the attack upon the Church; it is surrounded, closed in on every side, and the terrible storm is ready to burst, when the Defenders have the wisdom to capitulate; they march out with the Honours of War, and lay down their Arms at the Feet of their Conquerors."

44. The general Preliminaries and dispositions for the Attack of an Intrenched Village will be understood from this little Sketch of Proceedings, which is indeed no ludicrous perversion of the Author's meaning; and the points of Attack being selected, the Columns may be formed for the Assault on the principle adverted to in No. 6. The means to be pursued for overcoming the different Obstacles that may be expected to present themselves are likewise detailed in CHAP. III., but as much of what Old Sprightly tells us "is more easily said than done," it remains to add a few Practical Observations upon the Mode of Attacking the Chief Works, in which we may suppose the Srength of

an Intrenched Village to consist; which will bring us in contact with Fortified Houses or Churches, Redoubts, Flêches, or other Earthen Works, some or all of which may flourish as independent Posts, or form part of the contour taken up for the Defence.

Chap.— VII. Attack of a Flèche, or Earthen Work, Open in the Rear—a Redoubt, &c.

45. All detached Works, of the nature of a Flèche, that are said to be *open* in the rear, are usually so far *closed* that they have at least a good Palisading and Barrier Gate to shut them in: *au reste*, they are generally Earthen Works having Ditches of a breadth and depth varying with their importance, either revetted or finished in slopes, with a palisade in the bottom. The rear, however, is generally the weak point, and it is left open, in order that it may be defended from some other Work which sees into it. To assault such a Work, if it is of considerable size, several Columns of Attack may be formed; the principal one, however, should be directed upon the weakest Point, and it should be held in reserve, and if possible concealed, until the threatening attitude of the other attacks, (which may be directed on the salient or the extremity of either face) shall have induced a corresponding disposition of the Defenders; it may then come on, in all its Glory, and make short work of the Palisade, by some of the means before described in Chap. IV., the other Columns acting according to circumstances. If it so should happen that it was not expedient to attack a Work of this description by the rear, the general Plan of Operations would be reversed, and a show would be made of attacking that point, when in reality the principal effort would be made on the salient angle, or some other part, by a column kept out of sight until the attention of the Defenders had been previously engaged.

46. If the Ditch of a Flêche or other Outwork, is bounded by Walls, an Escalade with Ladders becomes necessary, for it is a long business filling up a Ditch, with bags of hay, or anything else, a dangerous one to jump into it, when deep, and an impossible one to get out of it when you are there, unless the retaining Walls are very insignificant indeed. If the Ditch is not revetted, but that still the slopes of earth are too steep for men to scramble up, Ladders applied to them will answer the purpose admirably, and if Ladders are not to be had, rough Steps may be made by Workmen, accompanying the Columns; all these Operations being under the protection of a strong Firing Party.

47. If Artillery forms part of the Force, a breach in the Parapet may be made with Shells, if time enough can be devoted to it, and the opposite Ditch being enfiladed to destroy the palisades, &c., a Column has only to wait for a signal to rush forward when these objects have been accomplished; but even in this case, with everything made so smooth, a false Attack, by distracting attention, could not fail to have a good effect.

41. The Attack on a Redoubt, which is a work enclosed all round with a Parapet, and supposed to be everywhere of equal strength, will be much the same as that of a Flêche. The angles are the weakest points, and the Attacks, whether false, or real, should direct their march upon them. A very sporting way of capturing a Redoubt is described by Capt. Macaulay, of the Engineers, in his excellent Treatise on Field Fortification. He says, "At the first blush of dawn a Troop of Horse Artillery should gallop up, unlimber on the glacis, and commence a rapid

fire of case shot to drive the Defenders from the Parapets; a Working Party carrying fascines, followed by a powerful Storming Party, advance at the same time with the greatest possible speed, the former fill in the Ditch enough to enable the latter to cross it, and enter the Work, which, if assaulted by good Troops, will certainly be overpowered."

49. As Facts, however, are more "stubborn things" than assertions, and are more instructive ones too, if experience is of any value, and as the former will make an impression, when the latter may fail in its effect, we cannot do better than give an example of such an Attack as has been under consideration; nor can one be selected better adapted for the purpose of exemplifying what judicious arrangement and vigorous execution will do, than Sir James Kempt's Assault upon Fort Picurina, a strong Outwork of Badajos, in May 1812.*

"*Description of Fort Picurina.*

"Fort Picurina is a Work in the form of a Bastion, of nearly 200 feet Faces and 70 feet Flanks, the Rear being closed by a front of Fortification. The Profile from the bottom of the Ditch to the crest of the Parapet measures about 30 feet in height, but only the lower 14 feet of the Scarp is perpendicular: at that height a row of Fraises was fixed on the Wall, and the remainder of the height of the Profile was gained by a Slope, which men could ascend. The Counterscarp measured generally 9 feet in depth; and at the rounding before the Salient angle of the Faces, four splinter-proof Casemates had recently been finished, which

---

* Jones's Sieges.

ASSAULT OF FORT PICURINA.

flanked the Ditch before the Faces. The Rear or Gorge was without a Counterscarp, but was well flanked from its Trace, and well secured by a treble row of inclined Palisades. The two Flanks alone were without Flank Defence.

"Within the Work, three splinter-proof Casemates, loop-holed, and having their entrances well secured, served as a retrenched Guard-house. (See Figs. 5, 6, & 7.)

"There were seven pieces of Ordnance mounted on the Ramparts, and the Garrison, commanded by a Colonel on the Staff, mustered nearly 300 men.

"Major-General Kempt, commanding in the Trenches, made the following arrangements for the Assault:—

"Two Detachments of 200 men each to be formed in the Parallel, the one on the extreme left, the other on the opening. Each Detachment to be preceded by six Carpenters with cutting Tools, five Miners with Crowbars, and 12 Sappers carrying Ladders. Lieutenant Stanway, R.E., to lead the left Column, and Lieutenant Gipps the right Column; and both Detachments to quit the Parallel at the same moment by signal. The left Detachment to move round the right Flank of the Work, and endeavour to force in at the Gorge. The right Detachment to move direct upon the Communication from the Town to the Picurina, and leave there 100 men posted, to prevent any succours being sent to the Fort; whilst the other 100 should be marched upon the Work to assist the left Detachment in forcing the Gorge, and prevent the Garrison escaping. A third or Reserve Party of 100 men, to be conducted by Captain Holloway, way formed in No. 2 Battery, in readiness to assist the other Detachments by a Front Attack, should they find much difficulty in forcing in at the Gorge.

ASSAULT OF FORT PICURINA.

"*Execution of the Assault.*

"It was 10 A.M. before these arrangements were completed, at which hour the signal was made and the Detachments advanced. The Left Party reached the Gorge of the Work without being discovered; but on attempting to cut down or force over the Palisades, the Defenders opened such a heavy fire of Musketry, that no one could effect it, although the utmost resolution and perseverance were displayed by both Men and Officers.

"The Right Detachment strictly obeyed its orders, and the half of it which proceeded to the Gorge of the Work were received with such a heavy fire, that after two or three fruitless attempts to get over the Palisades, they drew round to the Left Flank of the Fort, where the Ditch was not flanked, and fixing their Ladders against the Fraises projecting from the Escarp, the foremost were quickly on the top of the Parapet overlooking the Garrison defending the Rear. The French Troops on the Ramparts immediately concentrated to oppose this effort, when a spirited conflict ensued, and those first up the Ladders seemed likely to be beaten back.

"Whilst the contest at the Gorge was still doubtful, Major-General Kempt ordered the Reserve Party to advance from No. 2 Battery. It entered the Covered way at the points where the Palisades had been beaten down, descended the Counterscarp, and applied the Ladders to the Fraises. The foremost men readily mounted, and waited on the Fraises till some 20 or 30 men assembled; when they pushed up the Parapet, but were so firmly received by the Defenders, that many were shot or bayoneted back,

ASSAULT OF FORT PICURINA.

and they only forced in at the same moment that the right Detachment mounted the Flank. Some of the Garrison continued to resist even after the Assailants were in possession of the Ramparts, and were consequently bayoneted; and many were drowned in the inundation in attempting to escape; but a Colonel, two other Officers, and 80 men were made Prisoners.

"This brilliant Achievement cost the Troops four Officers and 50 men killed, and 15 Officers and 250 men wounded. Captain Powis who commanded, and Captain Holloway who conducted the Reserve Detachment, were each badly shot on the Parapet, of the Left Face of the Work; and Lieutenant Gipps received a bayonet wound on that of the Flank."

Chap. VIII.—Attack of a Fortified Building.

50. The planning and execution of an Attack on a small Military Post, such as a Fortified Building, the defences of which were detailed in Chap. X., (Part I.,) will more generally fall to the lot of a young Officer, than the comparatively larger operations against a Village or Redoubt, &c.; but however small the Post may be, if it has been judiciously strengthened, and is ably defended, there is opportunity enough for the exercise both of talent and bravery in assaulting it. But let us have a fair fight with no Artillery on either side, so that we may see what has to be done, and how certain difficulties which are peculiar to the nature of such an operation are to be surmounted.

51. First of all we will suppose that the greater part of the information detailed in No. 2 has been obtained by an Officer meditating the Attack; that he has had his eyes and ears open; and that with the aid of a good Telescope, he has made himself, and those under him, well acquainted with at least the nature of the External Defences, &c. His points of Attack are selected, and we will imagine that the little Garrison is "wide awake" to his intentions, and on the look-out to receive him; moreover that he has a fine sunshine to enliven his proceedings. He divides his Force and forms his Columns of Attack, and the first onset is made on the principle and with the precautions already explained in Chap. II. We will suppose too that the Obstructions on the outside are surmounted by some of the means detailed in Chap. III., but here is a great staring

House now before him, barricaded and loop-holed from top to bottom, and full of people; and a very serious and inhospitable looking thing it is! If an Officer had not been able to procure accurate information of the mode in which this Citadel of the Post had been prepared for defence, (No. 3,) or that he had not sufficient knowledge of localities to enable him to arrange the whole of his plan of operations beforehand, it would be better for him, after a successful Attack on the External Defences, to throw his Force under any cover he could find for a few moments, whilst he took a glance at the remaining Works, and was making up his mind what was best to be done; otherwise he would have to risk a wild and uncombined Attack, which would probably entail considerable loss and might be a failure. It would therefore be his object, if possible, to Reconnoitre the House all round; but should circumstances induce him to to decide on directing his principal Attack against some part that he could see from the situation he had first gained, he might take his chance in trusting a false Attack on the rear, and leave it to be worked as seemed best, for diverting the attention of the Defenders, rather than lose time in being too particular. We will suppose that he is opposite an angle of the House, and under cover of some object within 50 or 60 yards of it, and that a little slope in the ground conceals his men when lying down. He observes that one side of the House is flanked by a Window and some Loop-holes which have been made in an angular portion of the same building, (B, Fig. 8,) and that on the other side there is a door in the centre covered by a Tambour, (A,) made of rough logs of timber set upright; the Windows on both sides are low, but a Ditch has been cut in the front to give height, and they are well barricaded with stout timber, loop-holes being left for firing through. He has brought with him six Ladders, 12 feet long, two Bags of Powder with Fuses attached, (No. 37,) and some good workmen with Axes, Crowbars, &c.

He resolves to attack the points A and B, because in closing with them he grapples with adversaries that are in a position to do him damage, if he remained at a greater distance. He divides his Force therefore so as to have two real Attacks in front, and one false one to threaten all the rest of the Defences, leaving a proportion as a Support, besides a small Reserve to apply as circumstances may require. (No. 29.)

He observes that if he rushes up in the first instance, directly for the angle of the Building, he will be less exposed to fire than if he faced either side, and he decides that this shall be his line; and as strong measures on these occasions are greatly to be commended, he makes up his mind to expend the two bags of powder, one in breaking up the Tambour at A, and the other in blowing open the Barricaded Window at B;—then to effect an entrance by means of his Ladders, through the Window A, and to force the door within the Tambour by a liberal use of Sledge hammers, and Crowbars. (No. 55.)

52. It is of course a great object not to expose men to fire, unless their presence or services can secure some corresponding advantage. He therefore determines only to send those men forward in the first instance who will be wanted for fixing the bags of powder and firing them, and a very small detachment to protect them during the operation, by watching any particular Loop-hole that may defend

ATTACK OF A FORTIFIED BUILDING. 65

the points A and B. To provide against accident he tells off two men to carry each bag, and two others with lighted portfires for firing them, each party to be accompanied by six men, so that any Loop-holes which bear upon the situations where the bags are to be fixed, may either be silenced, or at least have their attention distracted. The success of the operation appears to depend greatly on the adroitness of the men who have charge of the powder, and he therefore has selected some smart fellows who know what they are about, and points out to them what is to be accomplished,—how it is to be effected,—and what particular duty each has to perform. The Columns of Assault, too,—the Firing Party, and a Reserve to protect the Flanks, or fall back upon in case of accident, would all be told off, as well as the Party for the False Attack; but no movement should be made till everything was in perfect readiness. He would then explain the general plan of the Attack, and point out the position of the Reserve and Support, &c.; after which the Detachment for the False Attack might move off, going by the least exposed route to the rear of the Building. There they might amuse themselves, vapouring about a little, and would soon become engaged, which would not be without its effect; for the Defenders, from being separated by different apartments and floors, and their only look-out being through Loop-holes, would become unsettled as to real plan of Attack, from obtaining but very confined and partial views of what was going on; and as their duties require them more or less to conform to the measures that may be adopted in the Attack, anything, even the firing of blank cartridge in different quarters, would tend to disturb them, and at least keep those at their posts who might otherwise be advantageously employed elsewhere.

53. A favourable moment would be chosen for commencing operations. If there were any Cover at all, the Firing Party might quietly distribute themselves opposite the two sides of the House to engage attention, rather than with any hope of doing damage; for a Loop-hole is so narrow that it would require very good and very steady shooting, to fire into them from such a distance as we have supposed.

The Bags of Powder would now be dispatched;—the two Parties would make a sudden rush up to the angle of the Building, and then dividing, these would be nothing left for it, but to run the gauntlet as best they could to their separate points, either along the bottom of the little Ditch, dug to give height to the lower Loop-holes, or close along its edge. It is so difficult to "shoot flying" out of a Loop-hole, that they might laugh at the fellows grinning through them as they passed. All this would be the business of a minute or two. The Bag for blowing in the Window would either be propped up against it with a thick stick, or it might be laid on the sill. That for forcing out the timbers of the Tambour, might be hung upon a single nail, driven in at the time, or the loop would be thrown over the top of one of the timbers. The men for watching the adjoining Loop-holes should stand as close as they could to them, not exactly in front, but a little on one side, and keep up a constant fire into them, avoiding exposure as much as possible, either from the Loop-holes on each side, or those which might flank the place where they stood. It would be needless exposure of men, and the worst of two evils to make a general Attack on Loop-holes, unless under particular circumstances, where there was only one row, or that something had to be done, which would require a party to remain exposed for a considerable time. In cases where there were two or more rows of Loop-holes, and that the Defenders had the means of throwing Grenades, or rolling Shells down from the upper Windows, besides giving their fire, the means of Attack would not be commensurate with those of the Defence, and it would not therefore be prudent to attempt it, but on a limited scale; and when it *must* be done, Loop-holes may be successfully disputed by superior numbers, if you can get near enough to make pretty sure of firing in; the closer you are too, the less you are also exposed to any direct fire from others.

54. When the Bags were fixed, the Fuses would be lighted, and if the men could retire some 10 or 12 yards, or lie down in the bottom of the Ditch,—or as Bob Acres says, " by my valour," " stand edgeways," close against the wall between any two Loop-holes, till the explosion took place, it might possibly be more agreeable, and would be safer than attempting to go back to the spot from whence they came. At this juncture, the Axemen, the Party with the Ladders,—and one or both Storming Parties should be perfectly prepared for springing forward. The moment the explosion takes place, they should be up and away. If a flash of lightning were behind them, it ought to be " distanced considerable." The Ladders would either be applied to the Windows, as they would be in an Escalade; or if the Windows were low, they would be of service to form a kind of Bridge for crossing the Ditch, which might form the Obstacle to getting in. A Firing Party would

watch the opening, and the adjacent Loop-holes, and the Storming Party would resolutely enter, the moment the passage was ready, closely followed by the Support, which would at the proper moment advance from its place of concealment.

55. With respect to the Attack on the Tambour, some little delay might be necessary, as the Storming Party could not enter till the inner door was forced. The Axemen would therefore ply away, till they had accomplished its destruction, during which time other men sent for the purpose might recreate in firing through the Loop-holes, to assist in clearing the passage. When the door was forced, the Storming Party would advance, and by a vigorous charge through the opening, would overcome all opposition. The entrance gained, a momentary check to collect numbers might take place, and then a determined "cast forward" in pursuit of the Fugitives would be the right thing to do. If the Defenders were of a sort "not to be taken alive," and were "making play" for the upper story, where they would be more strongly posted, a sudden rush after them might afford the Assailants the opportunity of accompanying them up-stairs, and thus finish the affair at once. If the retreat were from one part of the house to another, they should be hotly pursued, without a moment for cogitation or taking breath, and they should be kept going till all opposition had ceased.

56. On the other hand, if the Defenders had succeeded in gaining the Upper Floor, and that the Staircases were either destroyed or too strongly barricaded to be carried by main force, a pretence at lighting a fire in the middle of the *Dining Room* would not be without its effect, or any

ATTACK OF A FORTIFIED BUILDING. 69

trifling preparations for making a Mine in the angle of the *Library*, if they did not fire down too much through the ceiling, so as to render it impracticable, would be as likely to bring them to terms as any measure which could be proposed. The smell of a little Gunpowder, or a Portfire, is never less attractive, and never has so adverse an effect on moderate nerves, as when it is connected with the idea of a Mine; so we will suppose, after these preliminaries, that the courage of the Garrison "oozes out" a little,—that they think better of it, and save all further trouble by an unconditional surrender.

57. If the lower part of a House were very stoutly barricaded, and that the Assailants were unprovided with Bags of Powder for blowing open the Doors and Windows, an attempt might be made to silence the Loop-holes which bore on any particular point, and workmen might be employed there in forcing open an entrance, either at a Door or Window, or in breaking fairly through the Wall itself. Or if Ladders could be procured, an Escalade of the upper Windows, which are not usually so strongly fastened, might be attempted; but if denied access at these points, we have not done with them yet; as Old Sprightly would say, "The brightest hopes remain for us." There is no just cause why the Roof should not be attacked. Ladders would be brought up and applied in the most convenient and covered situations that could be discovered, and, if possible, the Assault should be made on several points at once. Having gained the roof, Loop-holes might be first knocked through at a single blow, and made use of for driving out the Defenders: these would soon be converted into great breaches;—a few Grenades might take the duty

of a Firing Party in clearing the front a little; and an impetuous Attack from this perhaps unexpected quarter, would be likely enough to succeed. At all events it would be worth a trial, and "no man in England" has a right to turn his back upon a Post he is ordered to attack, from only *thinking* it is impregnable.

58. When people are "run to ground" in this way, nothing short of knocking under "*de haut en bas*" must be listened to on the part of the Conquerors; and supposing the diplomacy of the affair to have been done in due form, we will leave the Parties to smoke the pipe of Peace and "Caw me, caw thee" a little. If the subject of Attack were a Church, a Prison, or other large Building, the same principles and precautions might be applied, only with this difference, that the offensive measures would be arranged so as to keep pace with the increased means of resistance.

Specimen of ye Olden Time

Chap. IX.—Escalading.

59. Escalading differs in many important points from almost any other description of Attack, and as the difference is not so apparent at first sight as to be obvious to those who have neither had experience in the field, nor the advantage of witnessing, or being engaged in the practice of it, at Chatham or elsewhere, a little explanation of the *Practical* working of an Escalade, and of its *Principles*, may be acceptable.

In the Assault of Works, whatever their description may be, and under whatever circumstances, the Troops are usually formed in compact Columns; whether their efforts are directed against the Breach of a great Fortress, when this order is imposed from the front being restricted, or against the more extended Obstacles which cover the Defenders of Outworks or Intrenchments, which though not breached, may yet be assailable, the Storming Party is launched forth in Column to penetrate the necessarily thin line of Opponents, which are extended in array before it. And if this formation be general, we may fairly infer that experience has proved it to be the most advantageous order that can be adopted.

If to meet such an attack as this, the wings of the Defenders could be thrown forward to overlap the Flanks of the Advancing Column, it would be deprived of some of its advantages. For example, What occurred at Busaco? A great French Column advanced up a steep slope, in the finest possible style, to the attack of a Line posted just out of sight on the top of it; but it was charged, and as it were, wrapped up in a *winding sheet* by the 43rd and 52nd Regiments: the wings enveloped the mass, and it was almost exterminated by the close destructive fire that was brought to bear upon it. Now Troops drawn up for the Defence of a Parapet are more or less in Line, but they cannot manœuvre to any extent, and may therefore be regarded as Fixtures, and be estimated to the *In-coming Tenant* as such, and at what they are worth. Starting therefore on the assumption that a Line so posted should be attacked in Column, we will proceed to make arrangements for carrying it into effect by Escalade.

60. For the sake of illustration, a small case may be imagined, so that by going into the details, we shall see better what happens. Suppose an Officer, impressed with the value of a Column, and without experience in Escalading, to receive an order on a sudden emergency to go on with his Company, formed as a Storming Party to escalade an Outwork, having a Ditch bounded by a Scarp and Counterscarp Wall. A heap of Ladders are pointed out to him, and he may take as many as he likes; he finds them 18 feet long, requiring four men to carry them. His Company has been thinned down to 48 Rank and File, but they are all "good men and true." He says to himself, I'll walk into those fellows on the other side the Parapet, "like a flash of Lightning into a Gooseberry bush," and he draws up his gallant fellows in Column of Sections accordingly. He has nothing to do with Supporting the Attack: his object is simply to keep his Column together,— to get them into the Ditch,—and plant Ladders so as to enable him to attack the Defenders. His first impulse is

to order the leading Section to furnish themselves with Ladders, by which the Column shall descend into the Ditch, and afterwards ascend out of it. His Sections consist of only six Files, and consequently the 12 men in the leading Section would only carry three Ladders, which when planted side by side against the Scarp, would only admit of the three men who first got up, charging the Defenders, instead of the shock which he intended to produce by his six Files and their compact Quarter Distant continuations, which was his *beau ideal* of Assaulting in Sections. Another inconvenience presents itself: he finds that the three Ladders when taken up to be carried forward in line, also occupy a greater front than one of his Sections, and therefore the three men who first mounted, and all others who followed them, would be, on a small scale, in more extended order than he expected. He determines therefore not to give up his front of six men, at all events; so, to accommodate matters, he forms Subdivisions, and carries six Ladders in the leading one, which enables him to attack on the Front of a Section at open order; for the six men as they successively go off the Ladders, will be obviously on the extended front of a Subdivision. To pursue this for the sake of argument a little further:—if the Ladders were longer and heavier than we have supposed, it would require six men instead of four to carry them, and he would find in this case that the front on which a line of Ladders can be carried forward, is, as near as may be, that of a line standing two deep behind them; that is, three Files for each Ladder, or about 5 feet. Under this new supposition, to preserve his Front of six men, who would have to advance with 18 Files, carrying only six Ladders; but he is now supposed to be going on with four men to each Ladder.

61. When all is ready, the two Subdivisions advance, the Ladders being carried in line by the leading one, and we will accompany them to a little Storm of their own. They arrive at the edge of the Ditch, and lower their Ladders into it. The Men who carried them descend,—wait till the rear Subdivision comes down,—drag them across the bottom,—turn them over against the opposite side, and the leading Files begin to ascend, followed by the others in tolerably close order; that is to say, one man's head about on a level with his predecessor's heels. If they have luck they arrive in this order at the summit of the Revetment, and rush off the Ladders in succession, so that if the second man has still to ascend six steps of the Ladder when the first man springs forward from it, as the latter will certainly move over more yards than the former will accomplish feet, he will very soon be far ahead, and in the "thick of it" by himself. This is literally what must happen, from some cause or other, in nine cases out of ten. Here then we have the six leading Men charging over the Parapet, and braving the Bayonets of the Foe, the very worthy Representatives of 18 Files, the rest of whom *are coming*. These leading Men of the four, who carried and are to make use of each Ladder, and of the corresponding four who are to follow from the 2nd Subdivision, jumping down within the Work when the rear Files are only preparing to ascend out of the Ditch!

62. Hence arises a difficulty to contend with, in the loss of that compact form which it is considered so desirable to preserve in the Attack of Works, and which shows also the

difference there is in *physical effect*, between the well-supported onset of a massive Column, and the fragments of it, as they would come pattering on from an Escalade! In the one, the bayonet of the sixth man from the front, at the first collision of the hostile bodies, may be within 10 feet of his Adversary's breast, and in the other it cannot well be within 100. Here we are spread out into the worst possible form for making an impression ; we have neither *weight* nor *surface :* it is clear, therefore, something is wrong. A Column with a little Head and a long Tail, is like a " Newmarket Weed ;" and the one is as bad a thing for making an Attack, as the other is for " charging a Bullfinch."* How its shape is to be modified in the case of an Escalade does not yet appear, but it may be shown that *very* favourable circumstances are required to lend their aid before it can be accomplished, as will be considered further on.

63. But these two modes of Attack are not thus brought into invidious comparison with any view to depreciate an Escalade, but merely to make practice and principles intelligible to those who have not troubled themselves to on the subject. " Perish the thought" that an Escalade is to be cried down ! It is a SPLENDID ACHIEVEMENT, in

---

* There are many Gentlemen's sons, of considerable attainments, who may not be aware what is meant by this expression. In *this* sense a " Bullfinch" is not a Bird, but a growing Thorn Hedge, some 10 or 15 feet high, through which daylight scarcely appears ; and yet if a man wishes to keep with hounds in some countries, he must ride at all he comes across, at a full swing, and force a way through : to effect which the *Weight* of his horse will be all in his favour. A thorough-bred Weed would bound back from a good Bullfinch, as it would from the wall of Her Majesty's Jail at Newgate.

every way worthy of the brave hearts who may be sent forward to execute it. It has "*inter alia*" this great advantage, that it disencumbers a Force of a host of trammels, and renders them independent and at liberty to act and undertake operations under circumstances that would otherwise be insuperable. A Quarter Distance Column, charging as such, must wait for a Breach, or it must have Slopes that men can climb with facility; in fact, it must have a very good road made for it before it can act: add to which, the Attack is usually imposed at a *particular point*, which point, a determined Enemy will not only dispute, but will retrench and defend, with tenfold the advantages and obstinacy which he could a more extended and uncertain line of operations.

The successful Defence of the great Breach at Badajos, on the 6th of April 1812, will forcibly illustrate these remarks. By the work of a very few hours, a handful of French Troops were placed in a position to resist the efforts of the most powerful Column (certainly as regarded its composition, and probably its numbers) that ever faced a battered wall; with truth might the heroes who composed it have answered the shouts of defiance that reached their ears, "If we can't do it, who can?" Well might they have said so; for if *they* were brought to a standstill, the best Troops that ever trod the earth, could not have accomplished it under the same circumstances. Remember who directed them, and the weapon he wielded! That Breach was rendered impregnable to the Means at hand for forcing an Entrance. Not so the rest of the Defences: they were bravely Escaladed, and on a very limited scale too, and the Fortress was won by the performance of prodigies of valour, opposed to an heroic resistance. For whether we read the accounts of the British Assault, or the French Defence, we look over a page of Glory from the top to the bottom; and did not living Witnesses bear testimony to the Truth of the History now in our hands, and of what we hear from those who were engaged in it, there were Deeds done on that memorable night which are almost beyond belief.

The following spirited sketch of the Escalade of the Castle by the 3rd Division, given by Captain M'Carthy, (late of the 50th Regiment,) who acted on the occasion as Assistant Engineer, will convey a notion of it :—

"On the 6th April all minds were anxious for the 'advance,' and orders were issued for the attack at 10 o'clock that night. I again, with Major Burgoyne, R.E., attended by appointment General Picton, at 8 o'clock P.M.: General Kempt and several others were there. General Picton having explained his arrangements and given his orders, pulled out his watch, and said: 'It is time, gentlemen, to go;' and added emphatically, 'Some persons are of opinion that the attack on the Castle will not succeed, but I will forfeit my life if it does not!'

"The Division then entered the Trench, and proceeded nearly to the end of it, when the enemy's volcanic fire burst forth in every direction, long and far over the Division, and in every kind of combustible. The grandeur of the scene, as Colonel Jones says, was indescribable. Such was the appearance of the fire, raining from the besieged ; it was as light as day.

"When the Division had advanced some distance from the parallel, the enemy's fire increased considerably; I was walking between General Picton and General Kempt, when the former stumbled, and dropped wounded in the foot. He was instantly assisted to the left of the column; and the command devolving on General Kempt, he continued to lead it with the greatest gallantry.

"On reaching the front of the mound, I cried 'Up with the ladders!' 'What! up here?' said a brave officer (45th). 'Yes!' was replied; and all siezing the ladders, pulled and pushed each other with them up the acclivity of the mound, as the shortest way to its summit. The above officer, and a Major of Brigade, laboriously assisted in raising the ladders against the wall, where the fire was so destructive that with difficulty five ladders were reared on the mound, and I arranged the troops on them successively, according to my instructions, during which I was visited by General Kempt and Major Burgoyne; although this place and the whole face of the wall, being opposed by the guns of the Citadel, were so swept by their discharges of round shot, broken shells, bundles of cartridges, and other missiles, and also from the top of the wall, ignited shells, &c., that it was almost impossible to twinkle the eye on any man before he was knocked down. In such an extremity, four of my ladders with troops on them, and an officer on the top of each, were broken successively near the upper ends, and slided into the angle of the abutment;—dreadful their fall, and appalling their appearance at daylight.

"I was forced to the utmost perseverance of human exertion, and cheered to excite emulation. 'Huzza! they are long enough, push them up again!' On the remaining ladder was no officer; but a private soldier at the top, in attempting to go over the wall, was shot in the head, as soon as he appeared above the parapet, and tumbled backwards to the ground, when the next man (45th Regiment) to him upon the ladder instantly sprang over!!. If he was not killed, he certainly deserved a crown of glory. But so numerous were the intrepid, that the man above-mentioned could only be distinguished as one of the 'Bravest of the Brave.' I instantly cheered 'Huzza! there is one over; follow him!'

"About this time General Kempt was wounded: his exertions had been most arduous in bravely visiting, and directing every point of attack, through the heaviest fire!

"The Escaladers persevered amidst the determined opposition of the Besieged; and the contest at the Castle wall was desperate, the besieged throwing down broken waggons, beams, shot and shells, on the besiegers, and endeavouring to drag the ladders from the men below.

"Lieutenant M'Alpin, 88th Regiment, supposed to have been the first who mounted the Castle wall, was there killed. Several claimed to have been the first up; but so ardent were all to gain the summit, and spring over to the conquest, that it was difficult for the individuals to decide who the first was, as the intrepidity of our troops seemed to have increased in proportion to their difficulties, and to avenge the fall of their Generals, and of their numerous comrades who lay strewed around. It was indeed delightful to hear our buglers upon the wall near the citadel, sounding the animating 'Advance,' to proclaim their success, and accelerate the distant troops; which consoled the wounded, and ameliorated their pangs.

"One bold bugler, as soon as he mounted the wall—

determining to be first, when sounding the 'Advance,' was killed in the act of blasting forth his triumphal music.

"Numbers of heroes fell on both sides; at the Castle the bodies of the English and French laid upon each other; but General Picton's division conquered, and was established before 12 o'clock in the citadel, which commanded all the works in the Town, and enabled the other Divisions, which had been powerfully resisted, to enter the Town.

"The first person who entered was the gallant Lord Fitzroy Somerset, then Secretary to the Commander of the Forces, who, to ascertain the state of the 3rd Division, bravely forced his way through the innumerable obstacles and imminent dangers of the Town to the Castle, which he entered, and found the 3rd Division reposing in security."

But to revert to the subject; an Escalading Party wants none of the, perhaps impracticable desiderata, of Breaches and Roads, and adventitious aids, to Macadamise its path! It grapples with the Obstacles that separate it from its Adversaries, in all their pristine majesty and perfection, and as an Enterprise, it is out and out, the more sporting thing of the two; which is quite reason enough for its being "first favourite."

64. It may now be asked, if we are so "thrown over" when we attempt to Escalade in Column, what are we to do? Why Escalade in Line to be sure! Suppose an Artilleryman were so circumstanced as not to have a 24-pound shot to fire through an Enemy's Line, but had plenty of Grape and Canister; would not a bucketful of small Balls, directed so as to give a shower of Iron over their whole surface, do just as well? It is a question

whether it would not be much better :—the only precaution necessary would be to fill the bucket *quite full!* We must, however, turn from the Hyperbolic to the Practical, and look into the Details a little.

65. We see that it is impossible to preserve the massiveness and beauty of a Column in this mode of Attack. That no sooner does an Escalade begin, than out goes the Head of it into the Fire, whilst the Tail, flourish as it may, can render but little assistance. In looking for the remedy, it will naturally occur that if the Road across a Ditch were widened, greater numbers could at least be brought into action, and as NUMBERS will tell, in whatever way they may be applied, a partial remedy may probably be found: we will therefore deploy a Column, and try what that will do! Here we are in a form for really *charging* the Defenders, if they could but be got at; and though when mounting the Ladders again, the same cause will be found producing a similar effect, in spreading out the Line in open order as it did the Column, yet we gain the advantage of having Numbers to help us through, and the *resistance* to be overcome will not be in exact proportion to the *extent of surface* that is assailed. We have now hunted pretty nearly up to the truth,—for a right good Escalade should be a Charge in line. When, however, we come to scrutinise the executive part of it, we shall find, that though it is *Theoretically* a Charge in Line, it is *Practically* the rather bold undertaking of a cloud of Skirmishers, making an Attack upon a Force posted in Line on vantage ground, and standing in the best defensive attitude in which they can put themselves.

This looks awkward, and would hardly be attempted in

the Open Field; then what is to conduce to its success under more difficult circumstances? We answer, "*The pressure from without.*" The Fight is won by the resolution and audacity of Numbers, and by the employment of People who can harden their hearts, and keep their heads straight! And though these conditions are more or less essential to the success of any other mode of attack, yet they are all required in larger proportions for an Escalade, than for a dense mass moving forward in the shape of a Column. Some of the advantages of a compact formation are to be found in the human heart; men feel themselves more secure and better supported when *en Masse*, and are consequently less liable to the fatal panic which may attend a momentary check, or a *Coup Manqué*.

In the more open order which circumstances entail upon an Escalade, there is more opportunity of dropping behind, more probability of confusion, or something going wrong. Hence numbers and goodwill are the more necessary in the one than in the other. We want the *dash* and *activity* of a *Multitude*, to replace the *emphasis* of a *Mass*. If we cannot go through the Line, we must endeavour to knock it to pieces by such a "sprinkling" of blows as it cannot stand under. For better illustration of the subject, we will as before assume a case, but of rather a bolder outline, taking our leave of Escalading in Sections, and enrolling ourselves in the "*Anti*-single-gentlemen-running-over-the-parapet Society."

66. The Face of a great Outwork, 100 yards in length, is ordered to be assaulted by Escalade, with no restriction as to Men or Means! The Ditch is 18 feet deep on the Counterscarp side, and the scarp, or the opposite side, is 22 feet high; the Garrison 1000 men! "No restriction as

ESCALADING. 83

to Men or Means!" Here we are in clover!! Now Mr. Cocker, how many Ladders will that Face hold? putting them as close together as the men can carry them in Line, or as they can be reared all at once? Mind, all at once! And how long must they be?

Why each Ladder, to be carried without crowding, will require a good 5 feet for its own share. The Face is 300 feet: divide by 5;—that gives 60 Ladders to line it; we shall want 60 more to stand opposite to them on the Counterscarp side, in order that the Support may follow on, and the communication be complete. "*Tottle* of the whole," 120. And the length of each must be 25 feet on the Scarp side, and 21 feet on the Counterscarp side, for the ends should project some 3 feet above the Walls.* Very well! Now for the men to carry them, and who form the Advance of the Assault? Six men to a Ladder gives 360 for each Line, making 720 altogether. So far so good. We must now have another Line of 180 Files in Support, and another to that in Reserve; a Firing Party of 200 men in addition, and we will be content, not only to undertake the operation, but to bet odds on its success.

67. In making arrangements for such an Attack, the Ladders would be laid out in two Lines, with an interval of perhaps 100 or 150 yards between them, if it were in-

---

* This entails a certain amount of evil, but is recommended as the least of *Two*. The advantages gained by having the ends of the Ladders projecting above a Revetment, are—the increased facility with which men get either off them, or on to them; the better footing they gain; and above all, the *Time* that is saved by men stepping boldly off in an upright position, instead of crawling off on all fours. Against this obvious balance on one side, we must set off, the liability of the Ladders being thrown back by an Enemy, if he makes the attempt. But this the Firing Party ought to take care of; an Enemy coming *outside* the Parapet is a case of trespass.

tended that both Lines should advance at the same moment; or they might be as close together as was found convenient, if it were considered better that they should move on in quick succession. This latter disposition would be desirable, if the space on which the Party was to assemble were restricted, as it might be in taking advantage of any little Slope or Hollow of limited extent which might exist within a short distance of the scene of action, and thus favour the operation by concealing the previous movements; or if a Work were to be assaulted from a parallel at a Siege. Each Ladder as it lay on line on the ground, should occupy the same space as the three Files which are to carry it do, when also in Line, which according to the regulation distance or breadth of shoulders, will be a *good* 5 feet (we do not descend to inches).

68. This will do for the Ladders. We must now look to the best way of disposing the men for carrying them, which we shall find mixed up with the more important considerations which relate to the impression they are likely to make in assaulting the Work, and the subsequent formation, which should be attempted for securing the footing they may gain, so as to be in readiness to resist the secondary attempts of the Enemy, with his Reserve, to drive them out again. It will facilitate explanation to anticipate proceedings a little, and imagine the 60 Ladders carried by each Line to be already planted in the Ditch, and that the men who carried those against the Scarp, are beginning to ascend their respective Ladders, to make the Attack, (of course in single file,) whilst the others who carried the Second Line, are descending those on the Counterscarp side; in fact, that we have a noble road of about 100 yards

PLATE. II.

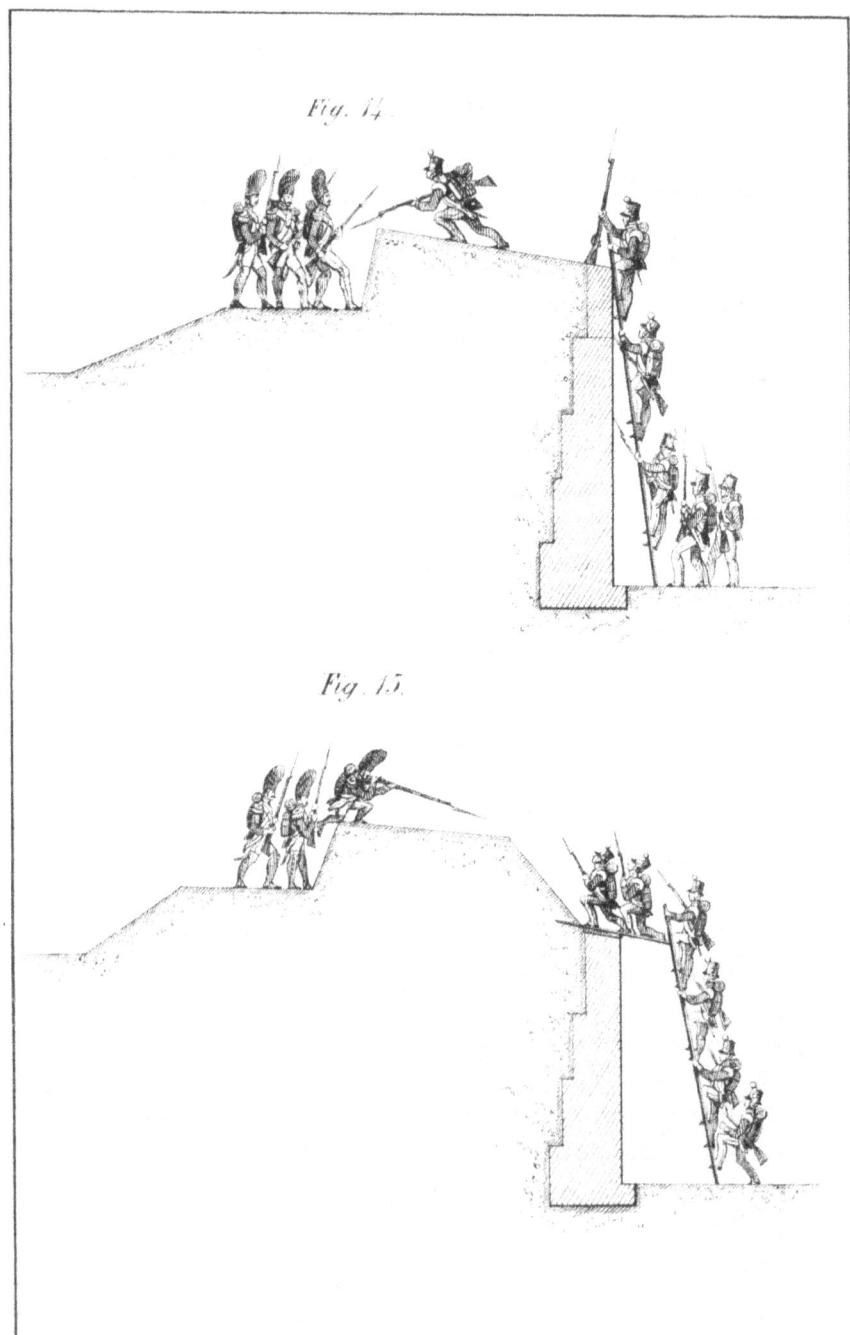

in width across the Ditch, and 720 men, " progressing" to the Fight. But in giving the Assault, what happens? Only 60 men out of the whole lot can advance abreast, so as to go over the Parapet and charge the Defenders at the same moment; and if their Opponents are drawn up three deep on the same Front they occupy, those 50 men in going straight to their own Front, with the intention of forcing their way and forming Line, again within the Work, would have to deal with 540—which is fearful odds, however quickly they might be supported. We will suppose, that from the form of the Profile to be Escaladed, (see FIG. 14,) no pretence at a formation can be attempted when the men first get off the Ladders, but that as they successively arrive at the top, they become exposed to a Fire directly in their teeth, and that they therefore rush forward to close with their Opponents as the best chance they have of beating them.

69. Now, without taking any account of confusion, casualties, and unavoidable delays,—and these items would doubtless swell the Bill a little, the very best order in which this Force could be brought to bear, assuming a regular and rapid succession for the sake of argument, would be in single Ranks of 60 men at a time, at extended order of three times their own proper front. The probable intervals between these supposed Lines might be something like 12 or 15 paces; practically it would certainly not be less. It may be estimated thus:—the Ladders are supposed to be 25 feet long, on which as an average it may be said four men are ascending at the same time; when the leading man arrives at the top, and gets a peep at his Adversary, he makes a rush forward, and if his strides are

measured, they will be found of vast dimensions, in comparison with the intervals of one foot between the steps of the ladders; and he is besides able to take two strides forward, whilst the next File behind him accomplishes one step upwards, from the cramped position in which the latter moves. In fact, we may fairly say, taking all things into consideration, that he would go *six* feet for *one*, or that the Leading File, if he had that distance before him, would be at least 12 or 15 paces from the Ladder when the second File got off it. This then is the distance we may assume between the successive squads that would come rambling over the top of the Parapet; and if there were not that, or a greater distance to move to the Front, and the intervals between the successive impulses were reduced into minutes or seconds, it would amount to a very appreciable period; sufficient at least for much to happen where it is "a give and take match," and when blows are dealt with a hearty good will on both sides.

70. It has been hinted that favourable circumstances are required for modifying the evil of the formation thus forced upon us, by the extended order in which the Ladders are necessarily placed, and the mixture of slow and quick time that is also entailed. These favourable circumstances will usually be found in the Profile, or form of the Work which is to be attacked; any footing afforded by a Berm or exterior Slope of a Parapet, not exposed to direct Fire, and on which men could make a momentary halt to collect numbers as they got off the Ladders—which might be done on such a Profile as is represented in Fig. 15, would go far to relieve us of our difficulties. In such a situation, the Berm and the Fraises together would enable the

PLATE. III.

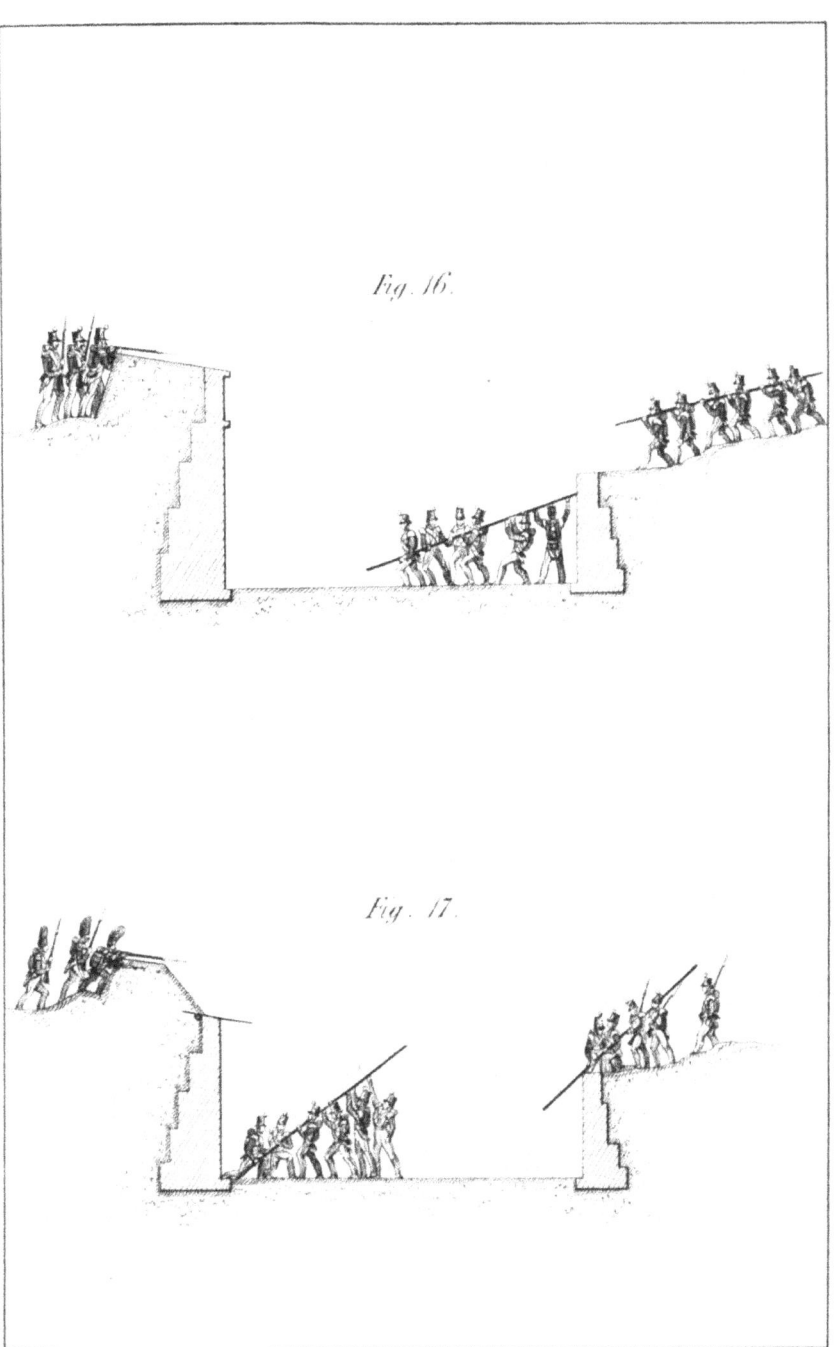

Fig. 16.

Fig. 17.

Assailants to form Line close under the noses of their Opponents, before they became exposed to their Fire, from whence they might charge them with effect; such opportunities, however, "are few and far between," but would be seized upon with avidity, as of obvious advantage.

71. When, however, men become exposed as they get off the Ladders, and that they must go on in succession as they arrive at the top, the difficulty of combatting their Opponents, and at the same time fighting their way into Line, would unquestionably be very great, in the loose order into which from circumstances they had been shaken. If the Defenders were to take to their heels, and allow us to say with Tom Thumb, " Thus far we've been victorious, for though we have not fought, yet have we met no Enemy to fight withal," it would be a different affair; but against a resolute and obstinate Defence, there would be a scramble for it. And sitting as *We* do in *Our* easy chair, speculating upon the issue, it does not appear quite so clear a case of success as it might be desirable to establish.

72. It is evident that in order to throw in *numbers*, the Ditch must be crossed on a very extended Front: in fact we must move in Line. But the question now arises, shall we continue in Line during the further operations that are in hand, or shall we make an attempt to regain the more compact formation of a Quarter Distance Column? The object is to make the Attack with every possible advantage, so as to breaking in upon the Enemy, seize the ground he stands upon, and afterwards to be in readiness to act as a Body *in the shortest possible Time;* either for resisting the efforts of his Reserve, or in following up success by sweeping the Ramparts or Interior to the right

and left, as circumstances might require. A compact formation will appear the more desirable, if we take into consideration the arena on which the struggle would probably take place, to wit, under many circumstances, on a confined narrow Rampart closed in Front, but open on both Flanks; than which a more unfavourable situation for a Line in disorder, being instantaneously applied with effect, either for further offensive measures, or for holding the ground it stood upon, could not well be selected. But we may scrutinise this point a little more closely, under the separate points of view which have reference, to the advantages it is conjectured would result from it.

1st. Is it better adapted for breaking an Enemy's Line, and forcing an Entrance, than charging *individually*, and then making the attempt to form a Line among the Enemy?

2ndly. Is the formation of a Column more likely to be effected, than that of a Line under the circumstances?

3rdly. When effected, does it secure to the Troops any advantages in acting offensively or defensively?

73. In reply to the first of these queries, whether a Column is better adapted for breaking an Enemy's Line, &c., reference must be had to the position and circumstances of the contending parties. It has been shown in No. 65 that an Escalade is analogous to a cloud of Skirmishers rushing in upon a posted Force. Now, however severely that Force might feel the quick succession of blows dealt upon its surface, it *ought not* to be overcome by anything like equal numbers applied in the open order, which an Escalade entails. This will be more readily conceded, if we for a moment change places, and imagine ourselves the

Defenders of a good Parapet, assaulted in such a manner. We shall fancy we could give a pretty good account of the aggressors, and "Bag" most of them, before they gained sufficient room to parade on our Rampart. We should laugh in our sleeves, and put a new interpretation on that tempting affiche one sometimes sees stuck up in a dirty window in London: "Single Gentlemen taken in and *done for!*"

74. If, however, we assign to the first few Files that rush on, the cheering title of "Forlorn hope;" or, if we regard them as Skirmishers covering the formation of a Column, which may be vomited forth in the confusion, at any moment, we shall cease to feel so very secure of standing our ground. It will be admitted that anything like a Column throwing itself upon a Line actively engaged in skirmishing along its whole Front, would be more likely to force a particular point, and establish itself, than were the same numbers to remain in an open, loose order, endeavouring to fight themselves into Line, when mixed up with a spirited Enemy, resolutely contesting the ground with them. The same remark will answer the second query: for to common sense, it certainly does appears that a Column would be more readily and quickly formed under such circumstances than a Line. With regard to the substance of the third query, of whether a Column established within an Enemy's Work, is in a better form for holding its ground, and being in readiness to act; a general view of the circumstances, and the confined space where the Force would probably be assembled, &c., seem to favour the opinion that a Column would be in every way more suitable for either purpose. It would be more in hand,

could move with greater celerity, and could certainly be applied with more decisive effect.

75. If the Principle be admitted, there is no difficulty in carrying the Details into effect, and in a very simple manner too. Suppose the Storming Party of the Escalade to be such as we have under consideration, viz., a Line of 180 Files, composed of six Companies of 30 Files each. We all know the advantage of *Rallying Squares* under certain circumstances, when men are in extended order: it is suggested to carry out the same principle in a regular manner by the formation of "*Rallying Columns,*" on the centre of certain distinct portions of the Line.

The Front on which this system of forming Rallying Columns on the centre could be applied, would be limited by circumstances, perhaps not in any case exceeding the Front of three Companies of 30 Files, or half the Force we have now in hand, but it would equally apply to the smallest Body. The arrangement of this point would depend greatly on the distance that it was desirable to form the Column beyond where the Ladders were planted; for it must be borne in mind, that with an Enemy in Line, close in front, the outer Files, in converging to a central point, would have to move along a sort of, gauntlet running, *hypothenuse*, to get to their places; and as a Flank march in front of a posted Enemy is not a pleasant operation, it would not answer to have too much of it.

76. In going into the Details for securing this point, and combining it with an arrangement for carrying the Ladders, so that the Companies may be kept together in both the Operations, which is very essential, we shall not do much violence to the principles laid down in "*The*

PLATE. III.

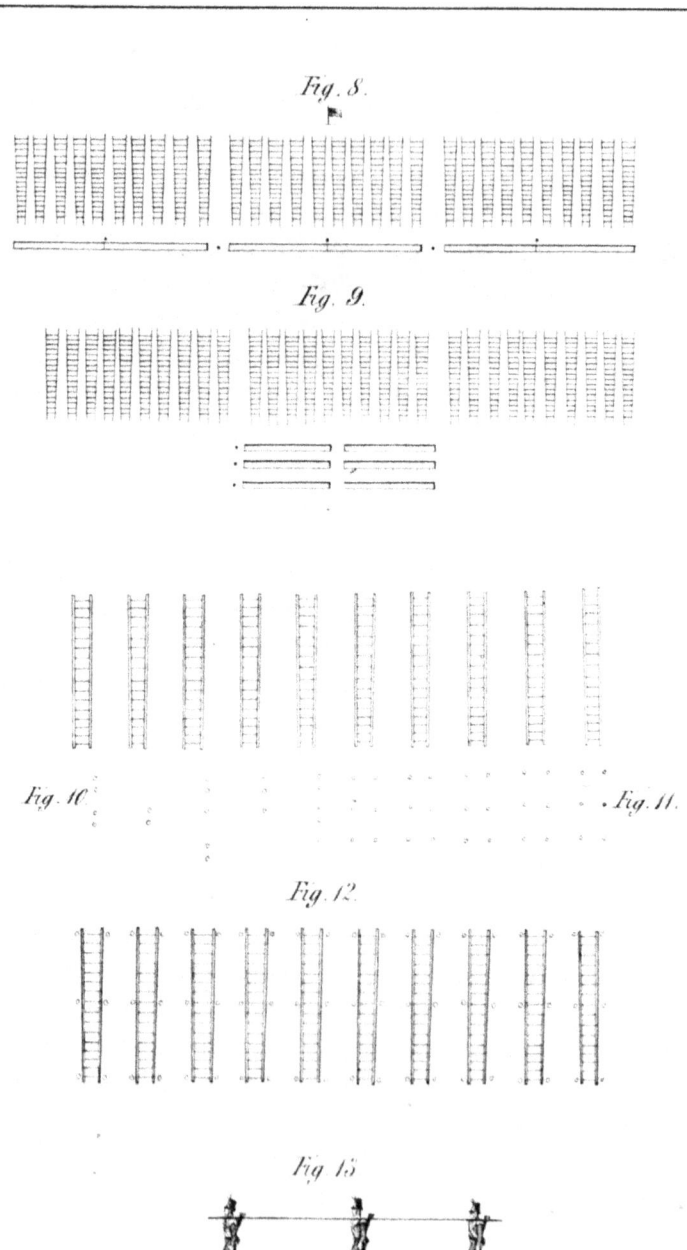

ESCALADING.

Book," which are on such a basis, that apply them as you will, the result will come right; we require a very little elbow room suited to the emergency, and that is all.

77. The object to be attained is already stated : we have three Companies in Line, and we wish to carry the Ladders forward, so that the Front Rank of the Centre Company shall be placed in a position to ascend the Ladders first, and afterwards to stand at the head of a Double Column of Subdivisions formed upon it,—we will say 20 yards in Front of where the Ladders are placed. The Ladders are supposed to be laid out all ready on the ground, in front of the Line (FIG. 8). The Cautions, and Words of Command, might be as follows :—

Form Quarter Distance Column, in rear of the two Centre Subdivisions. (See FIG. 9.) } According to Regulation.

By Files extend from the Centre, and Cover the Ladders.

Outwards face—or Outwards Close—Quick March.

} The corresponding Files of the three Subdivisions would Halt and Cover the Ladders in succession; the Ladders and Files having been previously numbered from Centre to Flanks.

The Files would then be in the position shown in FIG. 10, and the Rear Rank men would merely have to step up into the same alignment as the Front Rank, instead of Covering them, (as shown in FIG. 11,) and then being moved forward and filed between the Ladders, (FIG. 12,) they would be ready to advance with them in Line; and by preserving the order in which they then stood, or something like it, in ascending out of the Ditch, they would be in their places for reforming the Double Column again, in the situation required.

78. It may be said, this is all very fine and regular, but how is such order to be preserved under a heavy and destructive Fire? We answer,—the greater the probability of confusion, the greater is the necessity of taking every possible precaution to lessen the chance of it, and obviate its effects. It is not pretended that in the heat of action, men could exactly keep their places: the impetuosity and keenness of the many, and the *caution* of the few, would of itself prevent it; but every man would be in his *Right Place*, when at the bottom of the Ditch, for securing this formation; and they could not well be much out of it, in a compact Column of three Companies, formed within so limited a distance to their Front.

79. This explanatory digression being ended, we must revert to where it commenced, and suppose the two Lines of Ladders are laid out, and that the men disposed on the above system are in readiness to take them up. The most convenient way of carrying Ladders is on the shoulder, all the same as a coffin is transported, (FIG. 13); when, therefore, they were thus raised, the Line would be in readiness to advance, and in as close order as is practicable, which it may be observed *en passant*, is a point to be attended to.

The Firing Party would precede the Ladders, and act according to circumstances, the object being to keep down the Fire from the Parapets or Embrasures,—to prevent the Enemy showing himself, or making any attempt to throw the Ladders back, or in any way to arrogate to himself the right of assuming the offensive, outside the Parapet: any such attempt should be regarded as a decided case of trespass, and should be dealt with accordingly.

The Leading Division, on arriving at the spot, would lower the Ladders into the Ditch, (FIG. 16,) and the men would immediately descend, and when they were all down, would instantly shift them over to the opposite side, planting the foot of each Ladder against the bottom of the Scarp, and then turning the top over (FIG. 17); the foot being afterwards dragged away from the Wall about one pace, to give it a little inclination; but the less it has the better, for the more upright, the stronger it will be; and it is also easier for the men to ascend, than when there is much slope. The moment the first Division of Ladders were out of the way, the second would be lowered into the place from which they had been removed, (FIG. 17,) and the Men carrying them would in like manner descend; but those Ladders would not be shifted across the Ditch, but left where they were first lowered, and thus a complete communication would be established, by which the remainder of the Storming Party, and the Support, could follow in close succession, on the principle before adverted to in No. 6.

80. Numbers without mercy would thus be poured in; the outside Files still pressing in towards the centre, would consolidate into a Rallying Column, or *useful* Mass of some sort, in spite of every opposition; and if from the loose order in which the Leading Files became engaged, a momentary check was sustained on the top of the Parapet, it would only have the effect which Skirmishers ought to produce in Covering the formation in progress behind them;

and when there was weight and mettle enough concentrated at any one point, the opposing Line might be expected to give way before the moving Mass.

81. If the Front assaulted were extensive, several such Columns being established within a Work at the proper distance for deployment, would be ready to be applied in any way that ever-varying circumstances might dictate, and might be successively detached on separate duties, whilst the same formation was still proceeding, with any additional Force that might follow them.

82. If the supply of Ladders were limited, and it were necessary to preserve this complete communication across the Ditch for the above purpose, it would be expedient to have a greater number of Ladders raised against the Scarp than were left on the counterscarp side, because Troops when unopposed would descend into the Ditch faster than those which were already there, could ascend out of it, to the Attack; and thus the *supply* would be equivalent to the *demand*. The exact proportion that should reign between the two is not easily determined, and the readiest way of settling the point, is to say the "biggest half" in Front, and leave it to common sense and circumstances to decide on the spot, what shall be the precise limits of them both. In this case the larger division would be in the first Line, and the lesser in the second Line, and the Troops for Supporting the Attack would be drawn up on a Front to correspond with the number of Ladders by which they were to descend.

83. With a still more scanty supply of Ladders, or with greater means of resistance to be overcome; in fact where it would be very desirable to have the *whole* of the

disposable Ladders raised against the Scarp for making the Attack, we must not be deterred from the attempt by apparent difficulties. Send them all on in one Line if it *must* be so, carried by six men. Let another Division of men descend before they are shifted across the Ditch, and let the Support jump down upon bags of hay, as they did at Badajos! Throwing a Force into confusion, and letting men roll one over the other, will signify nothing in an Escalade, in comparison of the evil effects which result from breaking the ranks of a close Column on the eve of rushing forward to assault a Breach; *that* is to be avoided by every possible means. But with respect to an Escalade, there will always be delay at the foot of the Ladders; and if men get there at the time there is room for them to ascend, it is quite sufficient, and we must not, under the circumstances, expect them to come up in very regular order.

84. If we have still *less* than *a scanty supply*—never mind! Prince Hohenlohe is a fool to British Troops, when miracles are to be wrought, or impossible things are to be done! As a Specimen, let us take the Escalade and Capture of the French Works of Almarez, by Lord Hill, in May 1812. It was an Enterprise as conspicuous for the wisdom and foresight of all the previous arrangements, as it was for the boldness of its conception, and the brilliant manner in which it was executed. The following account of the operation, extracted from Jones's Sieges, cannot fail to be both instructive and interesting, and being most worthy of imitation, if ever a sword is drawn again, no apology is needed for stepping a little out of the way, to insert it here, as another standard FACT.

"*Description of the Works.*

"The Works at that place had been constructed with great expense and labour, by the French, under the view of securing their communication across the Tagus, on both banks. On the right of the River they consisted of a Redoubt for 400 men, on a very respectable Profile, called Fort Ragusa, with a masonry Tower in the interior, 25 feet high, having two rows of Loop-holes for Musketry.

"This Work being situated so far from the bank of the River, as to admit of the possibility of an attempt being made in the night to destroy the Bridge in its rear, a Flêche had been constructed on the River bank, which also served to flank Fort Ragusa.

"On the Left Bank, a well-flanked Tête-de-Pont, revetted with masonry on a good Profile, secured the Bridge; and as the ground rose immediately from the River to some Heights which commanded the Tête-de-Pont at a short distance, a Redoubt for 450 men, had been constructed on their summit. This Work, called Fort Napoleon, (Fig. 3,) had a Retrenchment across its rear, supported by a Loop-holed Tower in its centre, 25 feet in height.

"*Reconnoissance.*

"1st May.—This morning, Lieutenant Wright of the Engineers, was sent out to gain all the information possible respecting the Works, and the ground around them; whilst the Artillery Officers should renew their search for an opening to get their guns forward. The result of these examinations taking away all hope of forcing the Pass of Miravete, or of finding any other passage over the ridge practicable for Artillery, the Enterprise must have been abandoned, without some extraordinary decision on the part of its Commander. Happily that was not wanting, as will be seen below.

"*Movements of the Escalade.*

"At 9 P. M. the Troops began to descend the Sierra, and the Head of the Column arrived in the vicinity of Fort Napoleon at daybreak; but from the difficulties of the Road, although the distance from La Cueva did not exceed five or six miles, a considerable period elapsed before the Rear closed up. Luckily, however, some intervening hills admitted of the Head of the Column being kept concealed from the Garrison at about 800 yards distant; and the Troops remained undiscovered till completely formed. Soon after daylight, as had been concerted, under the expectation that it would be almost a simultaneous effort with the Escalade of the Forts, General Choune made a False Attack upon Miravete, and the 24-pound howitzers commenced a distant fire of round shot, and spherical case against the Castle. This Firing naturally attracted the attention of the Garrison of Fort Napoleon, and put them on the alert. They mounted on the Parapet, and watched with earnest curiosity the Defensive efforts of their comrades in Miravete, but did not seem to have the slightest suspicion of the blow about to be struck against themselves.

"About 8 A.M. the rear of the descending Column having closed up, the 50th Regiment, and one wing of the 71st, moved forward to the Assault of Fort Napoleon, regardless of a brisk Fire that opened on them, as soon as discovered. They descended into the Ditch of the outer

Work, at three points, and immediately reared the Ladders; but from the great breadth of the Berm, the Ladders could not be made to rest against the Parapet. Each Party, however, without being dismayed or confused, immediately ascended to the Berm, and took footing upon it; then drew up the Ladders, fixed them on the Berm as a second operation, and almost simultaneously mounted the Parapet, against a vigorous resistance.

"As soon as 15 or 20 Men were on the top of the Parapet, the Defenders of the exterior Line gave way, and made for the communication to the Retrenchment. This was by a narrow doorway, through a small Building covered by the Parapet of the outer line, from which a narrow Bridge led to the inner defence, and seemed to render it secure; but the Assailants followed the Garrison so quickly, that they entered the doorway together, and a sharp but momentary contest took place, in which the French Commandant was wounded and made prisoner. Overpowering numbers of the Troops having now escaladed the Fort, the Garrison abandoned the Retrenchment and the Tower, and fled in the greatest confusion to the Tête-de-pont, the Assailants pursuing them so closely, that both parties pushed together into that Work, when all resistance ceased."*

---

* After all, "there is nothing new under the sun." (See PLATE 4.) Look at y:̊ men of Ghent assaulting y:̊ Fortress of Dendremonde. There we see an apology for a Firing Party, attitudinizing with their Bows and Arrows. Here we notice a Lodgment for protection, only that it is *a moveable one.* There are half a dozen Ladders, and as many Men escalading a great Fortress. There are the Defenders ("striking with a deal of meaning,") and the Assailants, like honest men, paying them in kind. Brave hearts on both sides; and the same Principles in play centuries ago, which are now applied with improved details.

Ye Men of Ghent attacking ye Fortress of Dendermonde.

"The flying Enemy crowded on the Bridge to escape across the River, but those first over cut away three of the Boats, in consequence of which a number of Men and Officers leaped into the River and were drowned; and the remainder, above 250, were made Prisoners.

"The Garrison of Fort Ragusa, seeing what had happened, opened a fire of Artillery against Fort Napoleon, but Lieutenant Love most promptly turned the guns of Napoleon against Ragusa, and after he had fired a few rounds, the French Garrison evacuated the Fort, made a hasty formation at the foot of the Glacis, and then marched off towards Naval Moral.

"The reduction of these formidable Works was thus effected by means of the Musket and Bayonet alone, and with the loss of only two Officers and 31 Men killed, and 13 Officers and 131 Men wounded."

This is a history of what has been done with a scanty supply of Ladders; when, therefore, we have "impossible things" of this sort to accomplish, let us recollect what Hill did at Almarez, Picton and Kempt at the Castle of Badajos, Leith and Walker at the Bastion St. Vincente, and our hearts will swell with glorious emulation. The number of Ladders at the command of any of them was next to nothing; we have, therefore, only to follow the track that they have traced, and profit by the moral effect which the remembrance of such daring Deeds should inspire in the heart of a British Soldier, and we may then hope, not only to do our Duty, but to have our efforts crowned with the same Success.

www.ingramcontent.com/pod-product-compliance
Lightning Source LLC
Chambersburg PA
CBHW070202100426
42743CB00013B/3021